MW01200236

My Children, My Mission Field

A Family's Place in God's Plan to Change the World

Susan E. Field

New Hope Publishers
Birmingham, Alabama

MY CHILDREN, MY MISSION FIELD

*A Family's Place in God's Plan
to Change the World*

SUSAN E. FIELD

New Hope Publishers
P. O. Box 12065
Birmingham, AL 35202-2065
www.newhopepubl.com

Library of Congress Cataloging-in-Publication Data
Field, Susan E., 1957-
My children, my mission field : a family's place in God's plan to change the world / Susan E. Field.
        p. cm.
Includes bibliographical references (p.   ).
    ISBN 1-56309-731-1
    1. Parents--Religious life. 2. Parenting--Religious
aspects--Christianity. I. Title.
    BV4529 .F54 2002
    248.8'45—dc21
                    2002007529

Cover design by Cheryl Totty

ISBN: 1-56309-731-1
N034101•1002•5M1

To Taylor—
The best husband, dad, and world changer I know

Contents

Introduction

It all begins in a whirlwind of excitement and dread, pain and pushing, hugging and holding, smiling and weeping. Here you are, looking down tenderly at the red-faced, screaming, energized bundle of joy. All the longings of your youth, cemented by this great day . . . parenthood. You've now been ushered into the great fellowship of people who have nurtured, protected, guided, supported, loved, and raised children. You are contributing in a unique way to the values and choices of another whole generation. The tiny voice you hear now will one day speak according to your teaching. The little hands clenching and unclenching, waving wildly, will one day harm or heal as a result, in part, of the guidance from your hands. The tiny booted feet will go on paths, to some extent, determined by the vision you give them and show them.

These paths, mapped out by God before we're born (according to Psalm 139), are ultimately valuable to the kingdom of God. As you look on the precious faces of your children, visualize them walking the path God has laid out for them. Remind yourself of how much your own love for them mirrors the love of God for them and the love of God for you. "How precious to me are your thoughts, O God! How vast are the sum of them! Were I to count them, they would outnumber the grains of sand. When I awake, I am still with you" (Psalm 139:17–18 NIV).

Are you convinced? What do you picture for your children's lives? Prosperity? Princes, kings, and castles? Popularity?

Can you see them on a path that is dangerous? Lonely? Difficult? Sacrificial? Would you allow them to die for the sake of someone else?

The purpose of this book is to help you to visualize God's great and tender care for you and for your children, and to help you usher them into fearlessly knowing and doing what God has for them, regardless of the way things appear to us as humans. Imagine yourself climbing into the lap of God. From that angle, from God's perspective, you will be able to see with a much longer field of vision. Take time to commit yourself and your children to seeking out what God might want for all your lives. Be ready to shed fears and assumptions. Be ready to embrace total love and adventure.

The concepts, questions, and suggestions in this book are intended to provide a wide variety of possibilities for helping your family succeed as a family submitted and committed to God. No parent can possibly do all of these things or take in hand all of the issues raised in these pages. Just as there are many suggestions and actions described in this book, there are a myriad of family, economic, and social structures; emotional needs; and models for families. There is no single way to be God's pilot project for the world. In fact, one of the most important principles about God is that He makes us all unique and places us in unique families.

If as you read you begin to think more about "oughts" and "shoulds" than about "cans" and "oh boys," stop reading for a while and reflect instead on the freedom for which Christ has set us free—the freedom to care and to be part of a bigger purpose. Only you can decide how you and your family fit in to that bigger purpose.

The main goal of pointing out that freedom of Christ is to help families recognize God's special desire for them to know Him and desire to know His plan for them. The world will not change through any human plans or programs carried out by human effort, no matter how noble or how well executed. The people of God can only change the world by being close to God, trusting Him, and loving Him totally. Children will only come to God by having parents who love and trust the God who they are teaching their children about.

SUSAN E. FIELD

1
God and Me

If someone recommends a product to you, what is the first thing you want to know about it? "Did you use it yourself? How was it? Did it work for you?" Consider the faith implications this presents. Before you can trust your children to God's hands, you must first have a full assurance that your own life is safer and better off in God's hands.

In the Madison Avenue culture in which American children grow up, the truth about what people recommend is often unclear. Movie stars, experts, even doctors are paid to endorse products with which they may or may not agree. The children in this century will be the most wary and sophisticated when it comes to a sales pitch. That means if your own love for God isn't true, no amount of church programming, lesson teaching, or browbeating will convince your children to love God.

Psalm 9:10 (NIV) says, "Those who know your name will trust in you, for you, Lord, have never forsaken those who seek you." Parents who want to teach this concept to their children must first embrace it themselves. In order to gain assurance that can translate to your family, two beliefs are basic to following Christ, and you cannot pretend about these in the presence of children, fellow Christians, or God. One is: God is good. The other is: God is God. Nothing less than these two beliefs could allow caring parents to release their children from their own human control and give them the desire to see those children follow the will of God.

Evaluate
Before you read the rest of this book, ask yourself the following questions. Be honest about what you really feel. If you want to, find a notebook for your answers, as well as for notes and thoughts about the book. As you finish the book, look back at your initial answers to see if your perspective has changed about your family changing the world.
1. How would you describe God to a child under five years old?
2. What is the most important thing for a person to know about God?
3. How does God really feel about people?
4. What do you feel your life's purpose is? How did you come to that conclusion?
5. List five big events in the history of your marriage and family. Which ones relate to God?
6. What do you want your children most to know about God?

7. How does your family relate to others in your community? To others outside your community? To the international community?
8. What do you feel that your family's role is in God's plan for reconciling the universe to Himself?
9. What part does prayer play in your family's life?
10. How will you teach your children about missions?

God Is Good

Every Christian parent needs to understand with his or her whole heart that God is truly good. Our goal in knowing God is to trust God like Jesus did, not just to "be religious." The ancient Greeks and Romans in Jesus' day were very religious. They were devout and constant. They often worshiped with great sacrifice—crops, wealth, livestock, sometimes even their own children! They sang hymns and built incredible temples with wonderfully ornate altars. They celebrated feasts and festivals. They dedicated their children to their gods. But being religious did not put them in touch with the God who ruled the universe, nor did it allow them to become part of God's plan for humanity. It merely gave them calendars and rituals by which they could mark time. The rest of life was arbitrary, and sometimes very cruel.

The gods the ancient Greeks and Romans worshiped were invented. They were simply human characters living on Mount Olympus, given godlike proportions but showing human weakness. All of the emotions, vices, and problems in the human world made up the stories of the world of Olympus. The gods manifested their power by manipulation and strength, not wisdom or self-control. No matter how devout or sacrificial the people were to these gods, they were never assured of the gods' favor. These gods were not good. They were capricious, lustful, and selfish. They were not holy. They were just like us. They were short-sighted. Often modern-day religious leaders seem to worship a God just like this. Even some who claim to be followers of Christ describe a vengeful, raging God who is ready at any moment to destroy human beings who don't do the right things. Whole flocks of people are misguided into believing that the Christian God is a God of arbitrary wrath.

The God of the Bible, on the other hand, is a God of goodness, purpose, and vision. His guidance always leads to our good as well as God's perfect good. God's desire is that human beings prosper and remain happy on the earth. God created the earth as a setting for human beings to be loved and tenderly cared for. In fact, God's love is so great that He gave us the ultimate free-dom—the freedom to disobey. God's love was not manipulative or peevish. God loved us enough to give us freedom to make the choice to choose Him and fol-low Him, and He let his own Son, Jesus, take the punishment for our rebellion. What an overpowering love! What a model for us with our own children! Could we love them that much?

Imagine a courtroom, with yourself as defendant. In a fit of passion, you committed a horrible crime. The evidence is overwhelming and convincing. The jury finds you guilty. The mandatory sentence is death. As the bailiff leads you away, the judge stops the proceedings and opens his chamber door. There, already in prison garb, is the judge's own son. "Here. I have a stand-in willing to carry out the sentence of the convict. Let the prisoner go free," the judge says. In an instant your world changes from dark to light. Do you think the judge who made that sacrifice would then seek harm for you the rest of your life? Would you trust that judge with your next step in life, or run from the courtroom back into the activities that put you there?

A judge who sacrificed his own child for the sake of the defendant is not going to be vindictive, yet children in Christian homes are often taught that God is a cold authoritarian waiting to catch them at some bad behavior and punish them. A terrible epidemic of religiosity is being passed off for Christianity. People want the structure of Christianity—morality, ethical behavior, care for the poor—but they don't really want the cleansing power of God in their lives. The Holy Spirit, whom Jesus tells Nicodemus "blows wherever it wants to," is too disturbing for the people who want only religion. It's like someone who wants to keep clean, so they keep changing the baby's diaper, but won't put a new clean diaper on. They just keep repinning the old soiled one. But those who let God into their lives as a real and powerful force soon find that the ethics and morals and care for others are only a tiny taste of what the goodness of God is all about. They find power and security and incredible love. Those who let God into their lives find that God is all good and that religion is just the pattern we use for celebrating that goodness of God. Jesus never called His followers to "be religious." We are called to love God with all of our hearts and souls and minds. God is not somehow mad at us, waiting to zap us. He is waiting at the entrance to an exciting garden, open-armed, ready to love and care for us.

Christian culture has mistaken Jonathan Edwards's sermon, "Sinners in the Hands of an Angry God," to be the only picture people have of God, even those who know Christ's redemption. Sure, God wants to get hold of people. But not to punish them! He wants to get them and make them free from sin and guilt. Children who will follow God need to know from the earliest time in their lives that God is there to catch them when they fall, not catch them in a fall. As parents, we are the first to communicate this powerful love and mercy of God. Begin the influence you will have over your baby with all the assurance you can muster about God's goodness. Sing your children songs, talk to them, share with them that they are special and loved.

I was privileged to attend the *bris* (circumcision) of the son of a Jewish friend at my workplace. It was a great experience, and the most impressive part was the joy and welcome that everyone in the room had for the young baby boy. They sang songs in Hebrew and English; they read Scripture passages about how valuable and precious children are. They even posed the question "Will this be the Redeemer of Israel?" in one of the liturgies. I was touched and thought all day about how different the world would be if every single baby born on earth had this same joyful welcome into life. I imagined troops of singers and readers barging into hospital maternity wards all over the country welcoming all of the babies—from all socioeconomic levels, from all kinds of families, and in all types of situations. Even the orphans would be celebrated and cheered over, maybe even more than the babies with parents present. The experience of the bris was like an echo of the joy and excitement that I think God has at every new life, at every person's birth, regardless of what He knows their future will be. God rejoices in each of us and in our children.

Mercy, not punishment, is the story of Christ in our lives. And this is the story that our children will learn first from us. When you teach your children John 3:16, consider teaching them verses 17 and 18 also. Christ's mission on earth was to "seek and to save that which was lost." God is good, even though we are not good. We are to care for our families with this as our model. God cares for us and bears the consequences of our actions, even when we are rebellious and ungrateful. God has gone to great lengths to show us how much love and desire He holds for us.

Parents' love and desire for their children's good is not based on the good behavior of the children. The good parent loves through all kinds of responses. Knowing what forgiveness means to us, we are the first to teach our children that they can be forgiven. The children who recognize God's love will have seen your love for them, no matter what their behavior. But, they won't recognize the living God in a dead religion. And the parent who uses "God will get you" as their backup discipline tool needs to remember what kind of god they are expressing to their children, and how unlike the God of Christianity that is.

Consider:

- How are today's Christians sometimes like ancient Greek and Roman worshipers?
- When we're not at our best, how does our view of God sometimes mirror the temple builders?
- In your own life, have you ever made sacrificial actions with the desire to "win God over"?
- How can you begin to appreciate more the personal goodness of God in your life?
- What is your personal testimony about forgiveness? Will you relate this to your children someday?
- How can you communicate to your children, even infants, how much God loves them?
- What about parenting can you relate to the way God deals with us?

As you consider these questions, invite God, through Christ's Spirit in you, to "clean house" regarding your view of God. (If you don't know Jesus Christ personally, ask Him for forgiveness and acknowledge Him as your Savior. You can't "clean up" by God's standards without God's perspective. Pray that the Spirit of Christ will join you right now. Tell a pastor or Christian friend about your decision.) In the same way that you painted and scrubbed and decorated that nursery or that crib before you brought your children home, let Christ's light and love make a new dwelling place in you. "'You are already clean,'" says Christ in the Gospel of John, "'because of the word I have spoken to you. Remain in me, and I will remain in you'" (John 15:3–4 NIV). Open up to this gracious, loving God. Ask Him to help you trust Him, first of all with your life, then with the lives of your children.

Option for Action
Write a letter to each of your children, telling them how special and precious they are, and how much you and God love them. Put away the letter to present to them on some special birthday, occasion, or even when they are adults. Your testimony about your love will carry over beyond all of the day-to-day living in which we sometimes lose the sense of love and care. Any child will be thrilled and blessed by a tangible token of their parents' blessing and love.

God Is God
It is such a relief to appreciate anew how wonderfully kind God is. But to be wise and strong parents, we must also come to a whole new realization that God has the power to carry out His plans. God's resources will take care of any needs a person may have as he or she responds to God's call. Children can learn right from the beginning that fulfilling God's plan for them comes with the guarantee that God Himself will provide any resource or circumstance that they need for it to happen. There is no "martyr for God" in the sense of someone who does some mission all on his or her own.

God is in the midst of His missions, calling and supporting with His Holy Spirit.

In her book *The Christian's Secret of a Happy Life*, Hannah Whitall Smith tells the story of a loving and doting mother who has an adopted child. The mother is careful and conscientious about her child's life. She controls her environment as much as she can to keep her from harm. Still, she is anxious and worried about her. Smith encourages the mother to look at her worry from a new perspective. She challenges the woman to view herself from her child's perspective.[1] Should she worry that her mother will do her harm? If she obeys all her mother's directions, is she in danger of being ill-used and not taken care of? Will she fail to provide the food, clothing, shelter, or nurture that her child needs? How would this mother feel if her child constantly questioned her resources and ability to provide for her? Should the child ignore her care and run back to the orphanage, pleading for a place?

The example makes the point well. God's designs are for us. When we are called to obedience that seems severe, we are still in an environment controlled by God. People who know the direction of God in their lives can be confident that God will also provide everything their children need to prosper. Too often parents will sigh, "Well, I would serve God there, or in that way, if it weren't for my children. I need to provide for them, you know. If it were just me, I'd go in a minute." This attitude communicates to children that they are somehow responsible for keeping their parents from choosing God's will; or that if they weren't around, their parents would make more noble and faithful choices; or that God didn't figure them into His plans for their family. Think about what kind of God these remarks might invoke in the minds of children. It is not a fair picture of who God really is, only of who the parents see in God.

What a sad indictment of our churches and teachers when people use family as an excuse not to follow the direction of God! How could anyone consider that God is calling them, but not their families? And how will those families teach their children to follow God whole-heartedly? Parents who want to raise their children to be people of God must trust God absolutely. There is no way to believe, and at the same time "cover our bases" (in human terms). The two will conflict. God is much bigger than our bases, and children have a keen sense of when parents truly trust God.

For the Israelites of the Old Testament, this total control of God's was so overwhelming that they refused even to say—or write—the name of God. God was more than just a kindly, celestial "grandfather," who nodded with approval or frowned with disapproval as they did their daily business. God actively and powerfully gave them direction and set the course of their history. He took them through battles in weird and wonderful ways. He overcame their enemies; He fed them in the wilderness, and He provided what His people needed in miraculous ways.

Only when they veered from His specific directions or took actions to cover their bases were they left wanting. And often their disobedience caused terrible twists and turns for them in their history. God asked them to obey blindly, like Abraham; courageously, like Moses; with much physical expense, like Noah; in the face of poor odds, like Gideon; and in the face of social scorn, like Jeremiah. How exciting and inspiring to think that your message to your children is "My God is sufficient for me."

Consider:
- What aspect of God's control over the world is the hardest for you to accept?
- How will your view of God affect what you teach and show to your children?
- What view of God do most unchurched people have? How does that affect their parenting?
- In the example of the conscientious mother, what lesson did she need to learn?
- Do you ever fear that following God will leave you or your children lacking in the world? Whose view of lack are you holding up to God's provision?
- What purpose of God can you see emerging even from the worst circumstances in your life?
- Have you ever tried to "run ahead of God" to make something happen? Relate to your spouse, or a prayer partner, how it worked out.

Options for Action
- Gather the family together to talk about new and adventurous ways to trust God. Take suggestions from all parties and see if there are some creative and fun

ways that your family can let go of the world's ways and embrace Christ. One very real part of a believer's life is tithes and offerings. Decide as a family if there are new ways that God can use your finances to bring help and comfort to someone else or to your church (tithes first, Malachi says, "into the storehouse"; then offerings).

- Pray seriously together about a family direction—maybe some missions project or a new way to get involved at church. Make the focus hearing God, not doing more stuff. Invite children to participate in what they think God is telling them.

Parents or children who want to live out God's story fully must have an unshakable confidence that God is God, and that following God will lead to true happiness and success. Parents can pray and lead their children with the confidence that no other power, except our own lack of trust, can thwart the purposes of God. According to the Scriptures, God is not capricious and arbitrary the way other ancient gods were portrayed. His power is pointed toward reconciling the world to Himself. This should have a profound effect on every parent. Each baby, each child, each parent, and each life has an important part to play in the drama God is working out through human history.

Your own prayer life can help shore you up in times when you find it difficult to trust God's leading, and a constant and consistent prayer life will make those scary times much less unsettling. You will be used to the voice of God and the rebuke of Satan and his arrows of doubt and despair.

Who Am I to God?

As we learn to sort through our view of who God is, we also need to learn how God views us. Think back to the first play you were ever in, or to that first report or speech you made to a class full of peers. Perhaps butter-flies filled your stomach. Maybe you had sweaty palms and wobbly legs. Or maybe for you it seemed easy and natural. Whatever you felt, the experience forced you out of your own inner world into a public arena. Even if it was only your second-grade class, you were vulnerable to laughter and criticism, applause and affirmation, joy and tears.

Now think of your children. Imagine their lives thrust out onto the world's stage. What will be their part? How can you help them do their best? God's view of them (and of us) is the view of a Teacher, the Director, the Author. Our children are blessed to have a Teacher who knows not only their future part to play in the world but also their strengths and weaknesses. God knows what will make them shine and honor Him, and also what they will struggle with and what will trip them up. "'For I know the plans I have for you,'" God told Jeremiah. "'Plans to prosper you and not to harm you, plans to give you hope and a future'" (Jer. 29:11 NIV). God views us as His special people and as those who will help others know Him. Just as He initially called the children of Israel to be a "nation of priests" who would represent Him to others, we are also called to witness to the truth of God for everyone.

That same calling to groom us for our best part in life mirrors your role with your children, your "chosen ones." As you represent God to them, you teach them about their part to play in God's world. And as you teach them who they are, you have the opportunity to affirm them or shame them. Next to God, as a parent, you should know best the strengths and weaknesses of your children. This means taking time to fellowship with them and to respect and listen to their opinions. One wise mom said, "Children spell love, T-I-M-E." As you know your children, God will give you guidance about what special place they will have in God's plan. Be sure that you give them a legacy of hope and confidence, not feelings of inferiority or lack.

Gary Smalley's book *The Blessing* reminds readers of the importance of affirmation from parents to children and to healthy adults. We have a choice of being someone who blesses or someone who curses. Parents can be forgivers or condemners; they can live in a garden or in a desert. Conscious of these everyday choices, children can get all of the positive and healthy nurture that they need. And they will get a glimpse of the God who loves and cares for them and whose great desire is to bless them and see them happy.

Recognizing God's view of us, in light of the Scriptures, will change the views we have heard from the world about who we are and who our children are. One Christian speaker who deals with college students and their parents said that when he asks parents what they want their children to be, the most common reply he receives is "happy." That's all, just "happy." This is a common answer from Christian and non-Christian parents alike.[2] But just being happy is not our principal role in God's script. Happiness is a by-product of serving God; it is not a goal to be pursued for its own sake. It is a gift we get when we pursue God.

If we help our children recognize that God is good, that God is God, and that He views us with a plan for us in mind, they will have much clearer goals for their lives. And happiness will not be an illusive dream, suggested by every fad and sales pitch of modern life. It will be that voice of the Master saying, "Well done, good and faithful servant."

Consider:

- What are some parts that God has asked you to play on behalf of His kingdom? Are there ways to share how God has worked in your life with your children without overshadowing them?

- If your children are five years old or older, make a list of what you see as their personality strengths. Share these with your children. Be sure to praise them, and let them know that these are valuable traits that God can use for good. Teenagers especially need to hear things that they excel in.

- Are you (and your spouse) finding time to really know your children? Discuss ways to do this better, no matter what your work or stay-home context is.

- Think about how you have always felt God views you. Take time this week to be quiet and prayerful so that God can reassure you of His vast love for you. Perhaps God has some great new strength He wants to affirm in you.

Option for Action

How will you live out these views—your view of God and God's view of you? What impact do these have on the lives of your children?

The Book of 1 Samuel tells a great story about a mother who took God seriously and offered her son back to the God who had graciously allowed him to be born. First Samuel 1:21 to 2:11 provides a view of a mother who knew how gracious and powerful God really is. Hannah gave her much-longed-for son the chance to be everything for which God had created him! What a faith she acted out. Because of her awareness of who God was, and just who Samuel was to God, her son Samuel changed the course of much of the history of the Chosen People. By being the mission field for his mother, Samuel's life became useful to the mission of God.

A new option for Christian parents today is forming a "Hannah" group of like-minded parents. People who seriously want to seek God's control, direction, and protection for their children have a natural fellowship. While children play supervised in the next room, parents from your church or community can inspire and challenge each other about what it means to dedicate children to God. You can begin with a study of 1 Samuel. Believing parents can help each other recognize cultural norms that keep children from God's adventure for them. After studying 1 Samuel, the group can next look at the great courage of Abraham, as God called him to sacrifice his son Isaac (Gen. 22:1–19). Dads are called on just as seriously to give up the control of their children to God.

Consider:
- What do you need to release in your life so that your children can be dedicated to God?
- What realization did Hannah come to that gave her the power and peace to let go of the control of her only son?
- What knowledge did Abraham have that allowed him to tie Isaac to the altar?
- What are your goals for your children and their happiness?

---

[1]Hannah Whitall Smith, *The Christian's Secret of a Happy Life* (Westwood, NJ: Barbour Books, 1985), 21.
[2]Tony Campolo, speaking at North Carolina Baptist Men's Convention, Charlotte, North Carolina, March 1–3, 2002.

2

The World Around Me

Jesus loves the little children,
All the children of the world;
Red and yellow, black and white
They are precious in His sight;
Jesus loves the little children of the world![1]

Christian believers have a responsibility to learn more about God's view of the world He created and begin to see the world God's way. If we can transform our small, peephole perspective on the world into God's picture-window view, it will shape anew the way that we understand what God has for us, for our families, and for our children. The children's song above expresses a great and holy sentiment about Jesus' love for people of all races, but often our own view of the world is not as gracious about people who are different from us. To teach Christ to our children, we must tell them how Christ feels about all kinds of people. Our children will be loving and open to others, or will learn prejudice and a "soul smallness," depending on what our words and actions about others convey. The Bible teaches that "sweet and brackish water cannot come from the same spring"; and that "anyone who does not love his brother, whom he has seen, cannot love God, whom he has not seen" (1 John 4:20 NIV). Even the words that we use to refer to people of other groups are serious indicators of what feelings and prejudices are in our hearts.

My View: Looking Out

Nothing is more fun than watching the interactions of a group of preschoolers who have never met. They have no filters. You will hear played back, like a tape recorder, every word and political position and embarrassing confession their parents ever made (remember this if you have children this age). Without guile, but guided by what they have learned at home, they form very sophisticated social groups. Skin color, type of clothing, amount of lunch money, caregiver—totally arbitrary categories can put you "in" or "out" in preschool. At the same time, no group is so eager to please and so ready to get along with their peers, if they have some adult direction.

As you assess your work as a "missionary" to your children, think seriously about where you stand on issues of racism or nationalism. Is there a group or nation that you view as "on top"? Will you teach your children to gravitate toward (or away from) certain types of people? Paul addresses God's new way of teaching us to view others in his letters to the Colossians (3:11) and the Galatians (3:28–29). Does your Christian view of the world conform to what these verses say?

Another disturbing trend in the worldview of many faithful religious persons is the subtle, but deadly, attitude that "I am right and everyone else is wrong." Knowing that one has found the Truth and the Way and feeling definitely connected with God and His plans for the universe is not a cause for self-righteousness. It in no way reflects on how clever and sinless Christians are. It just means that God is gracious in His saving love. Paul, in the Book of Ephesians, reminds new believers that they are not too far ahead of the disobedient: "All of us also lived among them at one time, gratifying the cravings of our sinful nature and following its desires and thoughts. Like the rest, we were by nature objects of wrath. But because of his great love for us, God, who is rich in mercy, made us alive with Christ, even when we were dead in transgressions—it is by grace you have been saved" (Eph. 2:3–4 NIV).

God's goal for Christian believers is for them to reach out from helplessness and former hopelessness to those who are in the same position they once knew. Believers can be instruments of God's grace and mercy and can help people escape from God's judgment. Our calling is not to rejoice in assigning others to judgment. Thank God, human beings (other than Christ) are not meant to be the judges or the jury for other human beings. In fact, believers are commanded not to judge others.

How tragic when Christians are perceived as delighting in the downfall of others and when the image of Christ is someone who doesn't like sinners. "While we were still sinners, Christ died for us" (Rom. 5:8 NIV). That is the good news of the gospel. If children will learn this, and learn to communicate it, the world will change.

In the 1920s, the author A. J. Cronin wrote a novel about two priests.[2] One was smart and a good dresser, made great speeches, and was the favorite of all his seminary professors. He could pack in a crowd and host a great dinner for his superiors. But, "little people," like busboys and handymen and drivers, were not important to him. He used servants for just that—service. This priest rose quickly in the ranks of the church and was soon the head of a large parish. He was placed in even higher social circles and became even more upwardly mobile.

The second priest in the story is sincere, but not so bright. He hasn't had a life of social graces. He is not well liked at seminary because he seems always to be asking the questions that the professors can't answer. And, he won't answer with less than the truth. He is shipped off to a mission station in China and spends most of his adult life in a poor parish with few converts. But, he is loving and true to the people around him in the Chinese village where he serves. He is kind to all of them, even those who betray him. He renders medical help to one of the town leaders, but won't allow him to convert to Christianity merely as a sign of gratitude. His humble spirit wins over people in the whole region, who love and honor him for the rest of his life.

Which position would you want for your children, should they be called to missions? By the end of Cronin's novel, it is clearly the second priest who has hold of the heart of God in what he does. The first priest continues a life of selfishness and boredom. The story takes both of two kinds of success—God's kind and the world's kind—to their lifelong conclusions. Some people can show lots of success in sharing with others by numbers and statistics, but an air of paternalism and condescension pervades what they do. Other Christians share quietly and without fanfare, and the Spirit of Christ changes the world around them person by person. Only God knows the lives these people affect. They are not out to be compared with some standard the world imposes.

Mother Teresa, a nun in India who spent her life taking care of the poorest of the poor, knew the truth of a humble heart with no prejudice for or against anyone. It was her contention that Jesus did not take a statistical view of life. He cared for people one by one, individual by individual. She said, "I believe in person to person. Every person is Christ for me, and since there is only one Jesus, that person is the one person in the world at that moment."[3]

As you teach your children about love, help them to learn to embrace the whole world with love. Because God's love for them is unshakable, they don't need to feel inferior to anyone, or tear someone else down to build themselves up. Graciousness is the outflow of security. Your children, knowing their special purpose, can appreciate the special purpose God has for everyone who turns to Him. It is up to you to be true to God's view of the world and not buy into the human, incomplete view. God, the one true God, is seeking the heart of every person He has made, and people called to God's purposes need to know and teach their children that everyone is valuable in God's sight.

Consider:
- What insecurities in your own life have made you feel inferior to others? Have they caused a seed of exclusion or prejudice to grow in your life?
- What values about others have you communicated to your children? Do these values fall in line with the passages in Galatians and Colossians?
- What vision of your children as adults do you see? Are they in a group that looks and acts just like them?
- As you make choices about schools, churches, playmates, and sports, will you seek out a wide variety of types of peers for your children? Are you eager for your children to meet many different people from different groups?
- Is diversity important in God's plan for the redemption of the world? Does this fit in with your own view of the world?

Option for Action
If you live, go to church, go to school, or go to work in a racially or economically segregated part of town, make a plan to try and open up your children's lives to people who are culturally or racially different from your family. Find friends from other venues who come from different

backgrounds than yours—maybe from your children's extracurricular activities, from a club you may belong to, or from a friend of a friend. Be a host to other children who may not normally be welcome in your neighborhood. Express to your children how important it is to treat people fairly and kindly, even if they are different in skin color, income, or culture. Prayerfully consider what God may be calling you to do, in small ways, to conform the world to the image of peace and everyone worshiping the true God who is presented in Revelation 21.

God's Worldview: Looking All Over

Human beings throughout the ages have tried their best to understand about God, science, what we perceive, and what we sense. As you help your children grasp the realities of the world, and of this earth, an important key to understanding how things work is to remember that God is the Creator of the earth. It is important for children to know that, contrary to some popular teaching, it is quite reasonable to believe that our world was created by someone with intelligence and personality. The claims of physics and the theoretical sciences support this, as do some of the leading physicists. "Science" and "belief in God" is not an either/or proposition. The knowledge of and a relationship with God is, in fact, the key to understanding how the mechanics of the universe work!

Christians also have the responsibility to remember that we, as human beings related to God, were made the stewards of the earth. In Genesis 1:28 (NIV), God tells Adam and Eve, "'Be fruitful and increase in number; fill the earth and subdue it. Rule over the fish of the sea and the birds of the air and over every living creature that moves on the ground.'" Even though this charge was before the Fall, those who are reconciled to God through Christ have the insight and connection to God to once again become caretakers of the planet. How sad that in our present culture it seems that the witches and Satan worshipers appear to have a more tender regard for the health of the natural world than those who worship the Creator. How ironic that the ways and worship of those who follow the Deceiver will end in the destruction of life, while those who know the Creator will gain abundant life.

God has given His followers an earth full of ways to teach their children about who He is. Tiny butterflies, giant whales, puppy dogs, redwood trees—everything in nature points to how loving and magnificent God really is. His remark each day after each part of creation was completed was "It is good." No one should miss these tools that God has given us in our attempts to teach our children about His nature. It is loving and generous and relaxing and beautiful. Nothing in the world of human devices can speak as clearly to our human souls as the beauty of nature can. Children who know that they are part of a wonderful, created order of beautiful and good things will have a confidence that can change the world.

Consider:
• How do you really feel about nature? Is it annoying

and uncomfortable? What positive aspects about it can you teach your children?

• Think back about a special time in your life when you appreciated God as Creator. Describe it to a friend or to your children. What impact did it have on you?

• Why do you think the New Age and Wiccan believers present such an earth-loving front? How can Christians regain recognition as the earth's stewards? What actions can make you more earth friendly?

• How can you learn to see the world of nature through your children's eyes? How could they help you to know God better?

Option for Action

If you, like me, were raised in the city or the suburbs, a dose of "total nature" (like a wilderness or camping trip) can be rather daunting. Try to, with your children, face the fears of the things God has put on the earth for us. Begin by taking trips to the natural history museum or the botanical gardens with the family. Find the part in the nature puzzle that appeals most to you and to your children. Remind yourself and your children that God has made everything for the sake of the people He loves and cares for.

Lead your children in writing psalms and songs of praise to God for all of the great things He has created. Show them in the Book of Psalms all of the times that the psalmists (usually David) praise God for the created world. Help children to see that they too are part of this wonderful order and that God declared human beings to be good also.

God's View of People

Even though our limited minds are too small to know the fullness of God's view of the world He has created, God's thoughts in the Bible point out some of it for us. He is compassionate and forgiving. He helps those who cry to Him for help. "He is patient with you, not wanting anyone to perish, but everyone to come to repentance" (2 Peter 3:9 NIV). How sad it must be for God to see the sibling rivalry among nations, even among different Christian groups, as they struggle to be first. How sad when one group claims to use God's voice for the destruction of another group.

The New Testament Book of Ephesians gives us a good reminder of the way God views the world of Christians. Ephesians 2 explains how Gentiles (those initially outside of the Jewish world of Jesus) should now be brought safely into God's plan. As soon as someone feels like they are on the "inside," Paul reminds them in Ephesians that they were all on the "outside" before the sacrificial act of Christ on the Cross. It is just like the preschool class—everyone wants to be in, but left to our own devices, our criteria for accepting or rejecting someone are all arbitrary. Initially, we were all strangers to God's goodness, just like anyone outside of the Christian world. And any of us would stay strangers without God's grace and Christ's great sacrifice. Somehow, though, because of human insecurities, people like to paint the picture that they are somehow above others for having accepted Christ. Our view should be one of Christ who is above all. No human group or nation has any reason to feel self-righteous or to boast. We can only be "Christ-righteous"; nothing about ourselves can be righteous on its own.

A pastor living in the United States became a Christian as a boy under the teaching of a missionary in his native Panama. After college and seminary training, he was invited to come to the US to begin a Panamanian church. His testimony is a sad one. Having been nurtured and encouraged in his life with Christ by the American missionary in Panama, he was enthusiastic about his move to the States. He felt so much a part of the fellowship here.

Sadly, once he got to the US and made connections with pastors, his regional church group, and leaders in the denomination, he found that he was on the outside of whatever went on in a bigger way, outside his own congregation. No one offered to use him on boards or committees. He was overlooked and ignored at pastors' functions. Other pastors' wives snubbed his wife.

While this did not lessen his sense of calling, and he and his wife went on to build a strong, caring church, it is sad and embarrassing to think that Christians in what is touted as a Christian nation would not embrace a brother from another culture, especially one from the same denominational body.

As you set the stage for your child's view of the world, remind yourself and your family of God's great love for them. Remember, as God's servants, we are to represent His view of the world. Celebrate that God loves all people with the same incredible love and grace. There should be no joy to a believer that someone misses out on

God's forgiveness. Because you and your children are treasured and special, you can treasure and make special all the people God brings into your life. When your children find the "stream" of God's will into which they are to go, how joyful for you that that stream will be broad and deep, not shallow and restricted.

Consider:
- What "cultural protectiveness" did you learn growing up? Does it demean anyone or lessen your sympathy for anyone?
- Everyone in the modern world has some type of prejudice. Are you willing to make yours a matter of prayer? Can you submit to God your smaller worldview?
- Is there discrimination in your community or your church that has gone unchallenged? Prayerfully consider what actions God might want you to take on behalf of those who are unable to speak up for themselves.
- How will you address the idea of God's worldview with your children? Can you teach them in new ways about cultures and traditions that make all people valuable, to them and to God?

Option for Action
Empty a crayon box and refill it with crayons all of the same color. Invite your children to make a picture with crayons from that box. After you praise what they have drawn, ask them: If you had had crayons in different colors, could you have done more in your picture? (The answer will depend on the ages of your children.) Help them explore what other options come from having more

colors and sizes of crayons. Let your children know that God has made all different kinds of people on purpose so that He can make a great kingdom. Help them to see that God has a plan for everyone to play a part in the big picture He is making, if they will only trust Him. Teach your children that they have an important part to play too.

Consider:
Imagine for yourself the end product of God's kingdom—that final picture of earth, everyone totally working together under the bright sun of God's presence.

- What will that society look like to you? Think of what Scriptures, or teachings, have set the tone of that picture for you.
- On a sheet of paper, list the characteristics of the people in that kingdom. Also list the characteristics of ways that people will interact with each other there.
- Look at your list. Are you training your family to be citizens of God's kingdom?
- Does your list look too much like fantasy and not like reality?
- Make a plan now to train your children to live with an eye toward God's future. Jesus said, "The kingdom of heaven is at hand" (Matt. 3:2 KJV), but this can only happen if we cooperate with God.

---

[1]*The Broadman Hymnal* (Nashville: Convention Press, 1940).
[2]A. J. Cronin, *The Keys of the Kingdom* (Boston: Little, Brown and Company, 1944).
[3]"Great Quotations (Quotes) by Mother Teresa to Inspire and Motivate You to Achieve Your Dreams!"; available at http://www.cyber-nation.com/victory/quotations/authors/quotes_motherteresa.html; Internet; accessed June 27, 2002.

3
My Home in This World

One of the most incredible things your parents and Sunday School teachers probably never told you is how chock-full of love, lust, romance, and sexual encounters the Bible is. God and the people He chose to tell His message were very romantic, and many of the couples in the story of God's people loved each other incredibly. If you read the Book of Genesis, you find recorded for almost all of the patriarchs a love story between husband and wife that is explicit and celebrated. Although some Bible critics proclaim that women were treated as property and not respected in the Old Testament world, the Book of Genesis tells a much different tale. From Abraham, who loved Sarah, to Isaac and Rebekah, to Jacob and Rachel, to Mary and Joseph in the New Testament, the Bible holds up caring couples as the caring parents that make up the genealogy of Jesus. Surprisingly, many of these very loved wives were actually barren for many years, and were still loved and cherished by their husbands. God's miraculous work happens in the lives of couples who have a history of commitment to each other that extends far beyond procreation.

God Loves Loving

As you seek to usher your children into the kingdom of God, one of the most precious gifts you can give to them is a model for a loving and caring relationship between two married people. Children need to see that their most important significant others are carefully and intentionally holding each other dear, just like God holds each of us dear. A parent who cherishes his or her spouse will help raise children who will learn to cherish others.

Many times, especially in the lives of pastors, wives are the last to be cherished. Each of us can recount the tragic divorce or separation of people we know in ministry who have put their spouse last on the list of those to whom they minister. How sad for the children of those families and the level of trust that must have been broken with each other and with God. One woman, a new believer, once said of a divorcing pastor and his wife, "What I resent is that they acted so loving at church. I can't believe that a Christian couple could be so false in public. Why couldn't they have been more honest about their problems?" God's couples need to be sure that being a couple is important to them.

Even if you have lost the spark from your courtship

days, that spark can be recaptured by surrendering your relationship to God. God is a mighty matchmaker and delights in the love and affection a man and woman share through the marriage relationship. God, in fact, ordained the institution of marriage to be the basis for family. Psychology, social structure, child development, and healthy wholeness are all brought to their very best by the specific rules of marriage that God and Jesus set forth in the Scriptures.

Analyze your own childhood to understand the impact your marriage relationship has on your children. Were your parents really in love? Fond of each other? Tolerant of each other? Fighting? Maybe they were all of these. How did you feel? Which of these situations in your parents' relationship made you feel the most secure? When did you feel the most insecure? Some people's parents express genuine love to each other consistently. Others may never have seen an affectionate gesture or a kind word between parents. Some children never even know both their parents. As a couple, your responsibility to your children is to first love and honor your spouse, providing a safe, secure place for children to be the children. Often when roles or loyalties are confused, the children end up having to be the surrogate spouse, or even parent the parent.

In the same way that God has a plan for every child, no matter what circumstances brought them into the world, God has a plan for every marriage, no matter what circumstances led to it. Anyone who reaches out to God for help and guidance will find God more than willing to take control and make things good (often in the long term, not always in the short term). "'You will seek me and find me when you seek me with all your heart. I will be found by you,' declares the Lord, 'and will bring you back from captivity'" (Jer. 29:13–14 NIV) is the promise God makes to the people of Jeremiah's time. Sometimes that captivity might be a sour and angry marriage. God wants to set you and your spouse free from the bitterness and dissatisfaction of an unhappy marriage.

If your children are your mission field, the first place that they will learn about being loved and loving, cared for and caring is the example they see in you and your spouse. For this give-and-take of love and affection to last a lifetime (yours and your children's), the relationship has to have God's focus and purpose. You must be intentional and committed to the bigger plan that God has for the two of you, as well as your family. In a tender passage about friendship, the author of Ecclesiastes speaks of all of the advantages of two people together, but ends with, "A cord of three strands is not quickly broken" (Eccl. 4:12). The implication is that the two are stronger because of God's role in their relationship.

Consider:
- Are the patterns of relating to each other in your marriage healthy or hurtful? Are you able to recognize health?
- When was the last time you had a date (with each other)? What did you talk about? Was it really *fun* for both parties?
- Are there areas of conflict that you need to resolve with a third party present? Could you benefit from

some counseling sessions, even if only for the sake of the children?

- Have you specifically and intentionally asked God to bless your marriage and your household since your wedding day? Is it a regular prayer? Can you point to any specific results?
- Can each of you list five things that would really make you feel loved and cherished by your spouse? Will you share these lists with each other and try to carry them out as best you can?

Option for Action

Many people in the media and the entertainment world often say, "My family is always first with me," but schedules and appearances make that doubtful. This is also true in the Christian world of pastors, ministers, and seriously involved church members. If you are someone who makes that claim, you must be just as intentional with that effort as you are with anything you might do professionally.

Make a plan right now to strengthen your family by doing something especially wonderful for your spouse. Surprise him or her if he or she likes to be surprised (not if they don't!). Take your spouse somewhere he or she loves. Do something for your spouse that he or she knows you don't especially like. Treat him or her as carefully and preciously as Christ has treated you. Perhaps it is as simple as just giving your life partner your full attention for an evening, or taking him or her to dinner and a movie. Find time to let God, the real God of love, infect your marriage in new and exciting ways. "Do not withhold good from those who deserve it, when it is in your power to act" (Prov. 3:27 NIV).

NOTE: There is no question that for some people, no amount of wanting a good marriage to happen will make it happen. Whether caused by an unbelieving spouse, unhealed childhood wounds, mental illness, or simply an unwilling partner, some marriages will never be good environments for children. Whatever your situation, there is still hope in the God of love, who loves you and cares for you and your children more than anyone else. Begin now to pray earnestly for emotional health in your home and for your children. Claim God's promise in Romans 8: 28 (NIV) that "in all things God works for the good of those who love him, who have been called according to his purpose."

May I Have Your Attention?

A young mother with two preschoolers was having some trouble with her new role. She had quit a lucrative career to follow God's leading for her and stay home with her children. "I just don't know why they don't listen," she shared in a small-group discussion. "I do so much for them! We go to two play groups; I work hard to cook delicious, healthy meals; I read all of the child development journals; I keep a clean house. Why don't they hear me and do what I ask them?"

One member of the class, whose children were older, gently began to probe a little bit deeper. "What games do you play with them?" he asked.

"They have all the best educational toys and tons of software that they love to play," said the woman.

"Well, what do they talk with you about when you talk?"

"Oh, they're too young for conversation. It takes them too long to get anything out. Usually I'm busy with PTA or am trying to keep up with my friends on the phone. I'm sure they'll grow into meaningful conversation as they get older."

"What stories do you tell to them?" the man continued. He was hoping for some light to dawn in the mother's eyes.

"Every night I read a little of the children's classics to them. I figure it will help them once they get to school. They must like it. It always calms them down, and they are asleep before I finish."

The man shook his head. "Can't you see?" he said. "You don't know them. They can't trust you to mind you, if you don't really know who they are."

For many parents, coming from the busy, high-pressure, multitasking workplace means that every piston is firing in high gear. All of the competition and interaction that some parents have at work puts them in a completely wrong mode for children, especially young children. Many parents need to slow down and be "retrained" for work with young children. Children who will be led to Christ need first to be won over to love. They need to feel loved and valued, which takes intentional and focused attention.

A parent who is watching the children, basting the roast, ironing, talking on the cell phone, and listening to a CD is not, at that moment, parenting. He or she is simply "watching the children." Parenting takes slowed down time, imagination, interaction, praise, love, and value. To parent a child is to visit his or her world and use adult thinking skills to help encourage and interpret.

Jesus once told a parable about sheep and the shepherd as recorded in the Gospel of John: "'I am the good shepherd. The good shepherd lays down his life for the sheep. The hired hand is not the shepherd who owns the sheep. So when he sees the wolf coming, he abandons the sheep and runs away. Then the wolf attacks the flock and scatters it. The man runs away because he is a hired hand and cares nothing for the sheep. I am the good shepherd; I know my sheep and my sheep know me—just as the Father knows me and I know the Father—and I lay down my life for the sheep'" (John 10:11–15 NIV).

Under Christ's guidance, a parent is the good shepherd in a child's life. But, sometimes that shepherd can act just like a hired hand. Beepers, cell phones, email, Web surfing, cable TV, all of these are potential time robbers, taking your focus and attention away from your children. As communication tools and information technology get more and more mobile and omnipresent, everything becomes interruptible, even the most important times in your family's life. Although we don't admit it, we assign value by what we give our attention to for the longest periods of time. That means that the television, phone, and Internet may be more valuable in your life right now than the children you love and want to lead to Christ.

Think about someone whose love and attention you

crave. How do you feel when that person interrupts you to turn to somebody else? What do you imagine he or she feels about you when he or she leaves you alone in a room and focuses attention on a screen? How do you feel on the phone if someone puts you on hold to speak to someone else? Imagine how your children feel when you consistently cut them off to answer a beep or a page.

Even when we are taking seriously our good shepherd role, we leave our children in the care of other kinds of hired hands. Jesus' words ring true even for today, since the hired hands of children's television programming will not be there when your children have trouble or need comfort. An electronic baby-sitter won't recognize the wolves that can enter your children's lives. Commercials, witchcraft, foreign gods, "pocket" monsters, violence, magic arts, dragons, demons, materialism, secularism—these are only a few of the influences that appear quite regularly on television programs marketed to children. None of them reveals the truth about Christ and about the one God who loves all people. While they may teach your children reading or math or some other thinking skills, your hired hands also teach broadly about views of reality that differ with yours.

While you don't have to censor everything out of your children's lives (which then may backfire and give them much more appeal), you, as the "head shepherd," need to be aware of other influences and help interpret these for your children in the light of the gospel of who Jesus is.

Even Christian videos and CDs can rob your children of your time and attention. If you want them to know Christ and know you, you need to know them. Make it an adventure to explore this fabulous new world your children have brought into your home. "To have a child is to live life again," one proverb goes. If you are business-oriented, think of that child as a client. Be imaginative in how you will give your children fun and attention—things that appeal to you and to them. Enjoy knowing that you are the primary relationship for those little souls—someone completely new and different. Appreciate them so that they will know the love of God that has valued them since they were in the womb.

Consider:
- Do you have any set times during the day (or week) when you turn off all communication devices? Are you brave enough to use those times as playtimes with just your family?
- How do you interpret Jesus' story about the shepherd in John 10? Who do you think He meant by the hired hands in His day?
- How can multitasking enhance parenting? How can it be harmful?
- As you concentrate on spending focused, noninterrupted time on your children, think about a quiet time with God that can be just as peaceful. Talk with God about the many things you have to do and ask His help in finding time to share His love and appreciation for you and for your children.

Option for Action
Make one special time each week for learning about the world inside your children's heads. (Remember that as

they grow older you will not have this access, and they will have a need to keep private and individual thoughts.) Ask them what they think about a topic, get them to tell you a story they made up, give them a series of questions about what they like and don't like. Most healthy children will love telling you what they think and getting your approval. Do your best not to interrupt and/or correct them. Your purpose is to get to know them better. If you feel something is unhealthy or leading down a wrong path, gently suggest another option as a possibility. They are just forming opinions. Nothing is horribly (or perfectly) permanent.

Buy a special notebook to record all of these precious impressions and discussions. Use it in your prayertime to enlist God's help in knowing, appreciating, and praising your children. Give thanks for all of the ways your children are uniquely prepared by God for their own special lives. Pray that God will help you as you mold and shape your children's view of the world, careful to let them be true to God's design for them.

"This Plum Is Too Ripe"

In the off-Broadway musical *The Fantasticks*, act 1 reveals the romantic love story of two young people overcoming obstacles to find each other, fall in love, and marry. Act 2 begins with the song "This Plum Is Too Ripe." As the play "plays out," the characters must deal with the realities that begin to surface after the happily-ever-after part of the performance is over. It is a funny and poignant reflection on how life, and even love, can turn out to be something less than our hopes and dreams thought it would be.

For Christian believers, this ripening of life is not a huge surprise, nor does it signal a defeat for all of the hopeful and positive things to which our trust in God brought us. Christians are the most fortunate people because the God of the Bible is very realistic about sin and selfishness, and our God who loves us also knows us, even at our worst. As you guide your children into wisdom and an awareness of truth, you can teach them that God will help us face heartache, loss, disappointment, even death, with real power and faith. Not a denial of those feelings, God's comfort and the knowledge that He is in control gives us permission to feel real hurt without despair. As your children begin to explore life outside of the home you have provided (or even within home), they can have the tools to be "hard pressed . . . , but not crushed; perplexed, but not in despair; persecuted, but not abandoned; struck down, but not destroyed" (2 Cor. 4:8–9 NIV).

The reality that keeps a Christian from despair has at least five components you can teach and demonstrate to children from very early on in their lives. With these tools, they can face any hurt or trauma with courage and see real victory and promise in their lives.

1. *God's reality is much bigger than our reality.* Teach your children that God is Spirit, and that as Creator, He is bigger than just our planet. God's reality had no beginning and has no ending. We are promised that because of Christ we also get to live forever. So for the believer, physical death is just some kind of passage to

another type of life that God gives us.

2. *God promises that "in all things God works for the good of those who love him" (Rom. 8:28 NIV).* Even the worst tragedy can be redeemed in God's loving hands. From an early age children can know that God has a purpose for their lives and that His purpose cannot be thwarted by evil or by loss. If they remain true to God and cling to Him, they can be assured of God's victory and their own good.

3. *"There is now no condemnation for those who are in Christ Jesus" (Rom. 8:1 NIV).* Sometimes life's biggest hurts and heartaches come from the actions of those closest to us, and sometimes from our own selfish or sinful actions. Christians, especially Christian parents, can in a healthy way face shame and guilt and self-hatred because of the knowledge that God has forgiven us. Christ's sacrifice on the Cross makes us clean. And we live to do better through His indwelling Spirit.

4. *God's love for us is overarching.* Sometimes what we may perceive as disappointment and loss is really God's protection and love. Just like children, we sometimes want things that, in God's plan, are not healthy or glorifying to Him. God sometimes saves people from the things that they want because He knows that they are not the best choices.

5. *The Christian life on earth goes against the values of the world.* In some way, perhaps not physically, each believer will meet some opposition from the powers that control the godless world. Jesus said it plainly in John 15: if the world hates Him, it will also hate His true followers. While God does not cause suffering, He can use

it to draw people closer to Him and help them become more aware of Christ's extreme suffering on behalf of all people.

One of the most difficult things for nonbelieving friends to understand and accept about the church and about Christians is the perceived lack of trouble. "You're so Pollyanna," one nurse told me as I rolled in to give birth to my first son. And sometimes Christians do pose and pretend that all things are fine. "I've found the happy side of life," one church I attended sang together every Sunday. But no one mentioned the teenagers who were sleeping with each other, and the deacons who were blackmailing other members to get their way, and the money the secretary was quietly stealing.

God's kingdom must reflect a new sense of integrity and nobility, or the next generation of children will never go for it. And we can have this integrity and nobility because Christ has given us a way out of all the evil that can easily control people. Christians just need to become more transparent and more faithful in all situations.

Consider:
- Do you have any negative or sinful habits or behaviors you need to turn over to the forgiveness of Christ?
- What are your tactics when your children experience something difficult? Do you:
   a) shield them from knowing about hard things?
   b) explain to them what happened?
   c) get angry and blame others for rough things?
   d) try to find some comfort for your children in the Scriptures and through prayer?

- Try to think of some examples in your own life where God took a bad or tragic thing and made it into something that worked for your good. Spend time with your children to make these part of your family's oral history.

- What responses to bad circumstances did your parents model for you? In times of crisis, do you fall back on these behaviors? Are they positive or negative? What are some responses you feel you should work on to change?

Option for Action

Begin a chart or a journal as a family. You can use a timeline, a photo album, a notebook, or even an art file. Read Genesis, a chapter at a time, and talk together about the salvation history of the tribe of Abraham. Make sure that your family can recite its own salvation history as to how God, through Christ, brought good for all of you. If your family is too new to have any material, start with each adult and record what God has done in his or her life. Then, ask your children. Sometimes you will be surprised at how God makes Himself known, even to the youngest. Keep the chart or journal in an accessible place so that any member of the family can review it, even on their own. Make sure everyone can participate, even the nonverbal. Be sure they are represented so that later, when they are older, they can see that they were important and valued.

A True Home

Parents who believe in a resurrected and living Christ have an exciting job to figure out how to set their children on a path through the world that will lead them in a true way to the adventures that God has planned for their lives. In what is much like a puzzle, a maze, or even a video game, you are the "game master," making sure that your children have the tools and instructions to thwart the attacks that the enemy will make, trying to turn them from God's path. God's truth will inevitably run against the grain of what the world will try to teach your children about reality.

The world says either "Think for yourself, be adventurous, break the molds" or "Look out for number one, get what's coming to you, don't risk what you have a right to." One Christian mystery writer of a century ago described a life of following God as the antithesis to this. He said that it was all the adventure of a long voyage to new places, yet all the comfort and peace of finding that your destination turns out to be home.[1]

God set up the idea that a Christian home should have certain parameters and be based on certain values so that the spiritual realities at work in the world could be fully realized. The course of action that people choose does not determine what reality is, a popular concept in our culture. Reality exists, and we can only fully understand it when we have a connection to God, the Author of it. Scripture passages about what constitute "home" and "family," as well as the rules that govern the behavior of the people in the home, are laid out to help human beings live strong, wholesome, happy, and solid lives. Our culture wants to portray these rules as restrictive and oppressive, but family reality over the past few decades has proved the culture to be wrong. The concepts of home and family from the world's values have proven to be confusing and disjointed. People are more isolated and lonely, especially children. Roles and rules about healthy authority have been skewed beyond recognition. Reality seems to be the rock on which the baby boomer values are crashing.

The same author who wrote about the Christian life as a journey also wrote about God's rules for behavior. He said that there are rules, like walls, keeping people within certain boundaries. "But they are the walls of a playground!"[2] What a fabulous thought! How frightening it is for children to be playing at the top of a cliff, not knowing how close to get to the edge; not knowing where wild animals or danger might exist. How much better for them to be safe and unmolested in a guarded playground. The freedom and truth that were the ideals a generation ago can be found within the practical guidelines God gives in the Scriptures. But those who wanted to rebel against a false sense of religion pursued the ideal of "freedom" beyond all hint of responsibility or self-control. Christian adults who can set true guidelines and boundaries help their children learn to function freely and with more joy than those adults who expect children to make all their own decisions for themselves.

Many biblical principles make up the reality that God has throughout the ages tried to impress upon believers. Some of them help us especially in teaching our children to know God and how the things of God work in the world.

Consider:

- What do you think of when you hear the word *home?*
- How does your home compare with your ideal of home? What can you do to bring the two closer together?
- Make a list of all the traits of a family that you think are most important. For how many of these can you find a scriptural principle? Do they honor God?
- Pray about the nature of reality as it relates to your family. Is God a part of this for you?
- What new course of action could God use to further His kingdom in your life?

Option for Action

Like any good corporate exercise, people need to determine what their core values really are before they can decide what work to do and how to do it. With your spouse, and perhaps older children, try to record what you all can agree on as your family's values.

Remember the Sabbath

One of the realities that God instituted right from the beginning was the concept of a Sabbath rest. God Himself took a rest after creating the world and called it a holy day. The things He created in the world were all good. But, the day of rest—that space in time—was holy. Even before God gave the "Big Ten" (Commandments) to Moses, He showed us how reality can work best for us. We need time to be producers and creators, but we also need time to be absorbers and reflectors. We can understand what our lives mean only if we take time to rest and evaluate.

The Bible scholar Eugene Peterson describes it this way: "Sabbath-keeping often feels like an interruption, an interference with our routines. It challenges assumptions we gradually build up that our daily work is indispensable in making the world go. . . . [But, then we find] Every seventh day a deeper note is struck—an enormous gong whose deep sounds reverberate under and over and around the daily timpani percussions of evening/morning, evening/morning, evening/morning: creation honored and contemplated, redemption remembered and shared."[3]

One famous American Jewish scholar simply states that we need time to be the created, not the creator.[4] Because we know God, we need to know that we are *not* God, and that God can take care of His (and our) business in the world without us for one day a week. It is an exercise that is freeing and humbling at the same time.

Right now, imagine that you could be guaranteed 24 "free" hours this week. Think of all of the fun, relaxing things you would do, just for yourself. Imagine that you take on real Sabbath rules—no work at all. No cleaning house, no cooking, no lawn mowing, no phone calls, no beepers, no cell phones, no business transactions . . . nothing outwardly "productive." You could read a book, take a bubble bath, paint, play with the children, take a walk with your spouse, visit a museum, visit a garden, pray—anything that helps you concentrate on how good God is and how much you are loved in the world.

Does this sound like some unrealistic paradise? It's

not. It's what Yahweh God has commanded you to do, one day out of seven. It is an area where most American Christian churches have failed. Our "Sabbath" Sundays are more often less than reflective and involve tons of responsibilities and activities. Those who are committed to the life of their worship communities often have the least Sabbath rest. The joy and deepening that God wants for us has been folded into more of our frantic need for activity and action. Can a Sabbath rest be available to us in the twenty-first century?

If your family doesn't practice a real Sabbath of rest, begin to pray about how you can honor God in this way and enjoy the health that God meant for us in instituting the Sabbath. Remember Christ's words, "The Sabbath was made for man, not man for the Sabbath" (Mark 2:27 NIV). In other words, God does not intend for the Sabbath to be another oppressive set of meaningless rules to make you unhappy (or to make you feel like you are earning God's favor). It is for your sake that God forbids work on the day of rest. Peterson describes the two times God commands it: "The Exodus reason is that we are to keep a sabbath because God kept it (Exodus 20:8–11). God did his work in six days, and then rested. . . . The work/rest rhythm is built into the very structure of God's interpenetration of reality."[5] Peterson goes on to describe the Deuteronomic reason for Sabbath (Deut. 5:15) as related to the Hebrews and their life as slaves. For 400 years, they had to exist as property—almost as animals. Once they were freed, God instituted this time of reflection and worship as a sign that they were more than workers. They were God's precious creations.

As you think about a resting day, consider what a healthy legacy it will be for your children. Most of the top killer diseases in Western society are related to stress and fatigue. How many fewer bypasses would be needed if everyone took one day off out of seven? What do you think would happen to the collective blood pressure of America if this were the case? Imagine the value to your children, both mentally and physically, not to have to be "producing" all the time. Think of it as extending their lives and making them more delightful and stress free.

Were the Sabbath practiced by Christians more seriously, there would certainly be more poets and artists in the world! Perhaps the godly would be more influential to our culture and society because they would have deeper understandings and a deeper sense of who God is. The command of God about a Sabbath rest is a way to know Him better and in turn have a better and more godly impact on the world in which we live.

Consider:

- Is there another day in your week that you can turn into a time of Sabbath rest, from sundown to sundown? What other, shorter times can you commit to God through rest and reflection?

- Why do you think a Sabbath for us is important to God? What can a day of doing nothing productive teach us?

- Consider the main health problems of people in Western countries. Can you see a connection to 24/7 work? Can you admit that God's reality about who we are, and who we are not, seems to play out in our society?

- Are you brave enough to take this commandment of God seriously in your family's life, even if it goes against the grain of our culture? Would you take a financial or social "hit" in order to obey God about the Sabbath?
- Take time to think about the people who may work for you, or for members of your family. Are you allowing them a Sabbath rest? Do you think perhaps productivity could be increased if every worker had 24 hours off each week? Consider God's call on your professional life.

Option for Action

Before you can commit yourself to taking a day of Sabbath rest each week, you may need to study the concept and see for yourself why God made this rule. Take time to study all of the stories about the Sabbath in the Bible. Go to your church media library or local library and check out a Bible concordance. Look up the references for the word *Sabbath*, and keep a record of your study. Look up one reference at each sitting, and try to determine why God made this unusual rule.

Pay special attention to the times the New Testament records people breaking the Sabbath. Record any pattern you see. After you have studied the passages, spend time in prayer, seeking what God would have you to do about Sabbath rest, knowing your individual work and family situation.

[1] G. K. Chesterton, *Orthodoxy* (New York: Doubleday, Image Books, 1990), 10.

[2] Ibid., 145.

[3] Eugene H. Peterson, *Living the Message,* ed. Janice Stubbs Peterson (San Francisco: HarperSanFrancisco, 1996), 92.

[4] Abraham Joshua Heschel, *The Sabbath* (New York: Farrar, Straus and Giroux, 1975), 10.

[5] Peterson, *Living the Message*, 92.

4
The World Is Not My Home

Reality in the world that God shows us is often very different than the reality the media and our culture present us. Followers of Christ place value on very different things. Imagine that vandals break into a big department store in your town. Instead of stealing things, they wreak havoc by switching all of the price tags of the items in the store. The next morning, the store manager finds that a pair of gym socks has been marked at $500.00. But, a mink coat has a price tag of only $.50. The vacuum cleaners go two for $1.00, but the sponges are $25.00 apiece. Normal values are flipped on their heads.

In God's economy of things, this is the case. As you teach your children and build an intentional family, life becomes so exciting when you learn that God doesn't judge the way the world does (see 1 Cor. 1:25 and Matt.

11:25). Material circumstances don't dictate whether or not you are valuable. Jesus' life was never one of comfort or wealth. He didn't seem to be troubled by being born in a barn, or being "only the son of a carpenter." He had grace and courage and nobility; He had fun times at parties and strong friendships. All these are things we want for our children. None is the product of a bigger house, or a better school, or a particular car. They were by-products of parents who obeyed God unquestioningly.

These values are difficult to learn, but lead to an exciting and adventurous way to live a very special life. One Quaker writer tells us to not let our bank account make our decisions for us.[1] Think how freeing this is for you and for your family! First, it means not having to keep up with the people around you for homes and cars and gadgets and toys. God has a plan that fits you exclusively, and will always provide for you. You are freed from the curse of comparison, or feeling like your own worth is tied to the size or amount of your possessions. You are infinitely valuable to God. Your value is unrelated to what you have or what you earn.

Secondly, you are freed to find the gainful employment that God knows suits you perfectly. Whether your home has two wage earners or one, the jobs that support the family are also part of God's specific plan for your family. He can and will provide exactly what will "make our heart sing," if we will allow Him to guide us in this area.

Thirdly, we are free to pursue our ideals, and we can value the kinds of work and activity that the world doesn't value. We can be masterfully generous. We can relax and take a Sabbath rest each week. We can spend ourselves helping others. We can be the hands and feet of Christ without feeling like we're somehow not producing. As we learn to value these intangible things, we are also teaching our children to value the things that every society wants: honesty, generosity, helpfulness, kindness, and self-sacrifice. These are the realities that no one will deny are good, even though you will never see them advertised on prime time TV, touted in print ads, or taught in secular schools past the ages of nine or ten. We are valuable to God, and therefore are able to see the incredible value in others and to bring out in them their best. What a wild revolution there would be, if we could shake the sense that we somehow aren't enough for the world or for God and truly act like the princes and princesses that Christ's sacrifice has made us! Everyone would have a new view of his or her own reality!

This also helps parents as they evaluate what careers are right for their family and who should be the wage earner(s). Especially for mothers in Western society there are no easy rules today about who works outside the home, who works inside, who does the childcare, who does the housework. Everyone has a different expectation about what their role will be, and what their spouse's role will be. Often, young couples in premarital counseling are shocked to find out what their partner expects in a wife or husband. These are the fortunate couples—they are working things out ahead of time. Usually, couples don't find out about dashed expectations until after they have said the "I do's"!

Couples who are parents or hope to become parents should take time to decide what God is calling them to economically and how He has called them to make that happen. Prayer and communication can uncover what God has planned, but it also takes a sincere surrender on the part of both parents to live out that plan. God knows each of us individually, and He knows the synthesis our families will make (with our children and our future children). He knows all of the circumstances that will happen in the next several decades that we cannot possibly know. He knows exactly what part we were meant to play in His plan to make the world better.

In His knowledge of us, God has a plan to show us how this applies within our individual families. There are no rigid rules in the Scriptures about who "brings home the bacon," or about who nurtures the children, or in what way the job of parenthood is shared. The rigid rules are "one man, one woman, for life." But there are many models for parents' roles. Lydia (in Corinthians) is a homeowner and a head of a household. The "perfect wife" described in Proverbs sells purple cloth in the marketplace. From what we know in the Scriptures, Mary, Jesus' mother, kept the children and the house while Joseph supported them with carpentry. Naomi had to go out and gather leftovers from where the farmers had been. Dorcas did volunteer work and helped the sick.

The important truth about roles is that God does not allow any other gods before Him, so your economic decisions should be faithful and submitted to God's best. This means that you can sacrifice that second income, if

God is calling you to care full-time for your children. It means that both parents may need to work, if God is calling you to live where a second income is required. It means that you are free to sacrifice the material for the sake of the spiritual, and the great perk to this system is that God will only call you to the tasks that are most perfect for you! When you submit your life totally to Him, you are living out the fact that "life is more than food, and the body more than raiment." You are showing the world around you that your trust in God is the most important guide for your life.

Consider:
- What part of your marriage relationship causes the most strife? Is economics one of the top five areas of stress?

- If you have never done this, sit down with your spouse and discuss economic and role expectations that you have for your marriage. Even if you have been married a long time and think you know exactly what your spouse thinks, it is a good exercise to hear it from the other person.

- Is God calling you to a simpler lifestyle? Is your monthly income controlled by debts? How could you change the way your money works?

- Pray about the freedom of not having too much. Ask God to give you insight about how to honor Him, provide a healthy life for your family, and not be a victim of materialism.

- Think carefully about who spends the most time with your children. Be open to God's leading about caring for your children and what influences will direct their early and most important psychological development. Remember that the first three years of your children's lives can never be recaptured or made up for at a later time.

Option for Action
Plan a time for evaluating the values on which your family is built. First, meet together as parents. (If you are a single parent, perhaps this would be a good option to do with another single parent.) If you don't have children, you are in an even better spot to be intentional about the values on which you will build.

a) Write down the most important aspects of family life to you (each person needs to make his or her own separate list). Then compare. Are there any surprises? Did your spouse (or friend) value the same things you did?

b) Now, on the same page, write the top five goals you have for your family. Once again, compare with your spouse or friend. Are they similar? Are there surprises you didn't expect?

c) Together, discuss how much difference exists between your ideals and actual practices. What changes would move you closer to your goals? What do you value that isn't being intentionally woven into your family life? What is part of your life that doesn't really reflect the values you listed?

d) Next, revisit your values and goals in light of the Scripture. If you are not too familiar with God's Word, enlist the help of your pastor or a Christian friend you trust. Ask this person his or her opinion about the values and goals you have listed and how these mesh with God's Word. Take time to pray that God will open your eyes to see His unique calling and plan for your family. Thank God that He is with you in the desire to serve Him.

e) Finally, make a list of at least three things you will do differently as a result of this evaluation. Plan some fun way to celebrate the changes and assess what you have done.

Knowing Someone Versus Working for Someone

Think of all the times you have been employed. Did you have bosses? Picture those bosses in your mind. Were they friends? Relatives? Acquaintances? Did you ever have a boss who was distant and aloof? One of the realities in God's kingdom is that God wants us to know Him, not merely "work for" Him. The goal of the Bible and of Jesus' death and resurrection is that He can be the "firstborn of many children," not so that God can have lots of employees. God's heart is to redeem us, not hire us to do church work.

Knowing God intimately is more important than doing lots of "stuff" for God. Jesus' friends, Mary, Martha, and Lazarus, helped Him make a point about productivity and busyness. While Martha was working hard to get a good dinner on the table, Mary was sitting at Jesus' feet, learning about God with the other disciples. "Mary has chosen what is better," Jesus told the anxious and annoyed Martha (Luke 10:42 NIV).

Our children will be much more heroic and successful in God's plan for them if they take time to spend
with God and know His nature. Nothing will be more
frustrating for them than trying to please a God whose
nature they don't really know.

The classic novel *Scarlet and Black* tells the story of
a young seminary student who is a very hard worker and
very precocious. He is so talented, in fact, that he has
memorized the whole New Testament and is called on
over and over again at parties to recite, chapter and
verse, whatever people request. People marvel at his
devotion and his talent for the things of God. They
praise him over and over again as one of the seminary's
most promising students.

But, as the story proceeds, the reader begins to
understand the author's purpose. While the young man
is fabulous at his studies and can recite any or all of
God's Word by heart, his own heart is not God's. He is
prideful and selfish. He is not really the man of God that
people see in his actions.

Children face this same danger. As you teach your
family to love God and serve God, remember that it is
the *loving* that God wants most. No matter how many
Sunday School attendance stars your children have, or
how many verses and chapters they can recite at parties,
if they don't know God and love Him for themselves, it
doesn't matter. Devotion, not activity, determines
whether God is at work in the lives of the people in your
family. Of course, once devotion to God takes hold of
your life, the activities that God has for you will be part

of your life. But most of us get these out of order. Much more activity is done in churches *for* God than *with* God.

Once you can relax and love God and let Him love you, you may find that some of your Christian activity is not of God. It is important at times to say the "holy no," in your life and in the lives of your children. As a result, your children will grow up knowing how to hear God's voice and make appropriate decisions without the clutter and confusion of everyone else's voice telling them what they should do. Perhaps it is what Jesus meant in Matthew 11:28,30 (KJV): "Come unto me, all ye that labour and are heavy laden, and I will give you rest. . . . My yoke is easy, and my burden is light." God's main call to us is to love Him with our hearts and souls and minds. Activities and programs should only serve to enhance that in our lives.

Consider:
- Are the ideas presented in the above section new concepts for you? What did you think of as you read the story of Mary and Martha? Which woman seems to be the most like you to you?
- As you look at your calendar, are there obligations that are tiresome and tedious? If you pray about them, what do you think God will tell you? Which responsibilities (within the church and outside the church) do you love? What tasks thrill you the most? What would God answer in prayer about these?
- What as a family could you do to simplify the activity of life some? Are there activities that are unnecessary or unfruitful? Is God the author of your calendar and

time commitment choices?

- Evaluate your family calendar more closely. Are activities balanced between church/fellowship, family time, couple time, alone time, and time with non-believers? Each of these is important to a balanced life. Does your calendar reflect your devotion to God and to hearing His voice?

Option for Action

To understand the concept of being *with* God, instead of working *for* God, set aside a special time for each of your children. Give each of them their own day (or after-noon) of your time. Don't wash their clothes, mend their socks, or work on something else during their time. Just "be" with them, talking or playing a game. Let them decide what they want you to do with them. Ask them: Which did you like better, my spending time with you, or my doing household chores? Me talking to you, or me being busy cooking and cleaning for you? Think about how this could become a regular part of your family life, with each parent and child. Nothing communicates value to children better than undivided time and atten-tion from an adult.

There's More to It Than This

Real life, in God's definition of real, extends further in time than this earthly life. What a powerful realization, if we could make this part of our consciousness, and our children's. It is one way God has provided us with hope and courage and is a tool that God freely gives that allows us to do His will during this life. Death is for everyone, yet believers are then freed from death and live eternally with God!

We speak about this a lot in religious contexts, but do we "get it"? This gift is what enables Christian parents to send their children off to the mission field in total confidence. This is how you can be like Hannah and dedicate your beloved children to God. It is the reason that any of us can be brave and have enough love to lay down our life for a friend. Self-preservation is no longer our reality because God preserves our lives in Christ. "It is for freedom that Christ has set us free" (Gal. 5:1 NIV). Freedom from the fear of death trumps all other fears and freedoms. God has our good planned for eternity, and leading our children to accept this reality for themselves is perhaps the most important thing we can do in their lives.

Think ahead to the future. What will face your children in the way of war, disaster, or hardship? What terrorist threats are even now in the backs of people's minds? What fears are controlling the people you know? Fear is so unholy because it makes us forget the great and loving God who has our future in His hands. To allow fear to control your family's decisions is giving in to the ultimate weapon of the enemy; God's best is never allowed an opportunity to work. Fear negates the bigger will and purpose of God.

So, who is fearless? No one. Fear is an important part of survival and planning. But fear should be just a little brother—one voice among many, helping us make decisions. God's voice should be the ultimate ruler. Confidence in God's goodness and power should be the final deciding factor, not fear.

Along with the freedom from fear we can have in Christ is another reality that is often unpleasant to teach or try and understand. That is God's reality about safety. Who is safer, the man on the 35-story construction site walking on a six-inch beam, or the pedestrian down below, hurrying from intersection to intersection? What are the factors that make up safety?

In this instance, the man on the construction beam is much safer than the man on the street. The construction worker, up 35 floors, is harnessed and belted in. He is deliberate and cautious in his actions. He has performed the same task hundreds of times before and knows the dangers. He has confidence in his equipment and in his foreman. He would not go out on the beam tired or drunk or sick. He knows exactly what he is doing.

The pedestrian, on the other hand, is not totally sober. His feet are on the ground, but he hasn't bothered to look at a map to find out exactly where he is going. He is distracted, looking for addresses, not paying attention to the traffic. He doesn't have a clear picture of the place he wants to go. He bumps into people, making them mad, and curses when others bump into him while trying to avoid him. All of a sudden, a delivery truck slips through a red light and mows the man down, breaking lots of bones and knocking him unconscious.

These are pictures of today's families! Some look dangerously high, following God's leading, taking calculated risks, following a high calling and purpose, working for the Master at the task they were assigned, ready for whatever that involves. These are the families who are safe from the unknown and unexpected.

The second man typifies the family using the flow theory. This family plans on the basis of crisis. They operate on the firefighter model, moving from putting out fire to putting out fire. They are like the pedestrian running back and forth with a vague notion of where he is going, but not with an intentional plan to reach some specific goal. As a result they become cross and hostile and react unfairly to people they want to blame for the confusion in their lives. They will not be safe, in the reality of God, simply because they have not put themselves in God's hands to be used in His way. If we are Christians, our safest place is in God's will, even if to others the circumstances look unsafe. Conversely, if we take things into our own hands (and out of God's hands), we place our families and ourselves into very unsafe conditions.

Children who learn that God is with them will always feel safe and connected, even in the most frightening situations. (As a parent, you are to impart wisdom and prudence to your children. There are times for them to understand fears that protect them and to come to you for discernment and protection as long as they are children. They will not have the tools to decide about the dangers of different situations until they are grown.) The children who grow up listening for God's guidance will have the safest lives, even if their choices for God bring danger or death. They will not be defeated by death. They will truly be brothers and sisters of Christ and His resurrection.

Consider:
- What fears and insecurities are most frightening to you? Do they involve external things or internal things? (Remember that fears are normal; there is no shame in admitting them. In fact, we cannot surrender them to God until we admit them!)
- In the past, how have you dealt with your fears? What has been the most successful? The least?
- Commit yourself to pray about your fears consistently for one week. Keep a record of the insights that God gives you. At the end of the week, spend time in prayer specifically committing those fears one by one to God.
- What new perspectives for your family can the surrender of fears provide? What new actions can come from this new freedom?

Option for Action
Plan a family event that deals with fear. After some games and/or a meal, spread out some "scary" objects on a table or chair: a rubber snake, plastic spiders, a fright mask (the items will depend on the ages of your children).

Try to get your children to talk about fear and what they are afraid of. Be respectful, and help them know that you take seriously what they say and what they fear. Talk about whatever they mention. Use this time to teach them again how much God loves them and is in control of their lives.

Spend the final moments of this time in prayer for protection and courage. Teach your children a prayer or

Christian song that can be comforting when they are afraid.

Rising Up, Not Falling Down

Friends who are not believers in Christ (and some Christians) often have a great sense of disdain for the concept of original sin. "We're not bad! We're good!" people argue. "How could you think that everyone is evil? What about all the good in the world? What about good people who are not Christians? Are they going to hell? Are they all bad?"

Once again, Satan has twisted and used the world's perceptions about God to bar people from understanding God's reality. The truth of our sinful natures frees us to be good; it doesn't lock us into evil. It gives a rational explanation for the selfish and unkind things that people do and the rampant evil that can control parts of the world. As Christians, we are all fallen and forgiven. Out of the many great religions in history, only Christianity points out both the weakness of human beings and at the same time provides total forgiveness and the power of God Himself helping us rise above our weaknesses. In other religious systems, you must strive to earn favor from the god or gods; or you may strive for, but never quite be certain of, forgiveness. Or you simply do the best you can, taking into account the sins and hurts you are responsible for. The humility that comes from realizing our sinful nature as well as the loving redemption of Christ is a reality that will keep you and your children balanced and useful to God.

C. S. Lewis wrote a great story to illustrate the extent

to which people will go not to admit their sin and pride. In *The Great Divorce*, Lewis paints a grim picture of an imaginary group of people on their way to heaven. Most of them reject it simply because it involves humbling themselves in some way. They cannot rise up to greater things because they cannot let go of their own pride and will. If they could know their own blindnesses, they could be reborn to a new kind of sight; but they grumble and complain and prefer to stay in a foggy, unreal hell rather than admit sin and be born again in heaven.

Think of how freeing it is for us, and for our children, to know that we are forgiven when we do wrong! Rather than psychiatric excuses and sociological justification for the actions that are simply selfish and mean, children can feel so much more free by admitting what they knew was wrong, showing contrition, and finally being absolved and forgiven—by parents and by God. Discipline becomes just that, "discipling" rather than punishment. That discipline/discipling is not abusive because of the forgiveness and love that have already ruled the day and because Christ has already made the payment for the wrong in any of our lives. Parents can help their children learn consequences in instructive ways. They don't have to be violent or angry, meting out some payback on their children. God's mercy, the Bible says, triumphs over justice, and the reality of our sinfulness lifts us out of its control, into the noble and high calling of Christ in our lives.

Examine how your philosophy of discipline for your children reflects what you know as a believer in Christ. Are there connections? Most parents simply follow the model they had as children, trying to teach their children in the best way they can. Or, in cases where the parents had unhealthy and abusive parents themselves, there is often little or no discipline, and children aren't really taught the real boundaries that God has told us about. The Bible says clearly that "a good and loving parent will discipline a child," even as God disciplines us and teaches the path of truth (see Heb. 12:5–11). Disciplining children is not an "I win, you lose" kind of power play where we are trying to bend them to our will. It is a wonderful teaching privilege God gives us in which we are trying to produce people who will love and serve God with the rest of their lives. We are helping them form the internal controls that will be tools for them to use to be free and happy in their adult lives. We fail if we neglect to provide them with their own inner boundaries and force them to develop those boundaries on their own.

Although for the parent the responsibility to discipline can be difficult and unpleasant, it is the loving course of action in the long run. For example, the tantrum of a two-year-old over a lollipop at the store might be cute and even humorous. Certainly, the task of saying no and reprimanding that child, especially in public, seems especially harsh. But giving in and allowing the tantrum is much more of a harsh lesson for the child. When that child is five years old, that same behavior is no longer cute and funny. It is unruly and inappropriate. But the parent who has indulged the younger child now changes the rules on the older child, which is unfair. If the tantrum was rewarded with the object of desire, the parent is reinforcing the tantrums. One can hardly blame the child for what reality has been taught to him.

God clearly has a high regard for the moral abilities of children and what they can learn and handle about who they are. Jesus exhorts His disciples to come to God "like a little child," because He knows that children have an especially keen sense of what is true and what is fair. Although children can act selfishly, they rarely act with malice or guile. One has to grow up into deceit. The example we can share with our children about God's discipline is being open with them about how God works in our own lives to correct, guide, and forgive.

Consider:
- What is your feeling about the idea of original sin? Have you thought much about it at all? If not, ask your pastor or a trusted Christian friend what it means in your particular church. Does it change your perspective on people?

- Have you ever come to a time in your life when you realized your own sinfulness? If not, ask God to reveal to you His precious sacrifice on your behalf. Surrender the old nature to God, who can work in you a new and wonderful wholeness.

- As a Christian, what impact does the idea of "fallen and forgiven" have on your life as a parent? How is your role like God's role when you are dealing with your children? Will this change any of your practices? Surrender to God the way that you discipline.

- As you deal day-to-day with the children who are your mission field, what can you do to make them feel "forgiven, not fallen"? What positive aspects of their characters can you encourage, even as you discourage the negative behaviors?

Option for Action

If you are a parent, or hope to be a parent, discuss with your spouse your philosophy of discipline. Will you use corporal punishment? Will that accomplish your goals? Remember that inherent in the method is a teaching lesson (for example, spanking a child for hitting someone. It is hard for children to know where the difference lies).

Discuss the methods your own parents used, what you saw as effective, and what you saw as ineffective. If you need to, consult books and/or articles that give good disciplining insights.

If your children are old enough, let them participate in the discussion. You may be surprised to find out what is effective for them and what is not. They will feel respected and important if they are part of the process and will be more submissive to the consequences that they have helped establish.

---

[1]Richard J. Foster, *The Challenge of the Disciplined Life* (San Francisco: HarperSanFrancisco, 1989).

5

God Is in the Tent

John's Gospel records Jesus telling His disciples that they must "abide" in Him, that He will abide with them. The word Jesus used means "to pitch a tent with them." As we nurture our families, we have the honor of knowing that God Himself, in the form of the Holy Spirit, lives with us, right in our homes. While this is disturbing news at those times when we act selfishly or thoughtlessly, in reality it is a great comfort. The one who holds the world in His palm like a hazelnut[1] is there ready to help us with all His power in building our healthy and strong family life.

My husband's family sometimes lived this out very literally. At one Christmas dinner his parents set a place for Jesus, along with the five children, the parents, and the grandfather who lived with them. One of the youngest of the group, my husband forgot himself and burped loudly during dinner. In horror, he had to watch as his bigger-than-life father turned to the empty "Jesus" plate and said, "Please excuse my son. I'm so sorry," then turned back to the family and continued with dinner.

While this story is now comical, it made an impact on my husband about the Lord "dwelling with us." He remembered not to burp at the table again! And, he developed a real sense of the seriousness with which his parents took their commitment to the Living Christ. For them, serving Jesus was more than just trips to church once or twice a week; more than tired old Christmas stories pulled out once a year. Jesus was just as real as they were in that household. The important difference between Jesus and other leaders of world religions is that Jesus still lives today in us. It is important for your children to know this and to see it demonstrated in your life. And the fact that the Lord of the universe lives with you is even more powerful and exciting.

If believers fully realized that the Spirit of the risen Christ lives with them, the course of the world would definitely change. First, Christians would most likely display more courteous and respectful interaction, and the worst behavior would be minimized. But, more importantly, the family could get to know Jesus more intimately. Once conscious of His presence and His will for us, all of the day-to-day actions of a household become filled with meaning and purpose. How would Jesus treat others? What would He do for guests who come in? How would He discipline? What would He bring into the house for entertainment and amusement? What books would He read? What TV shows would He watch? Knowing the presence of a living Jesus in your house makes that adventure of being redeemed and treasured by God an everyday reality and makes anyone connected with your home a part of what Christ is doing on earth to draw people to Himself.

Consider:
- Are there things around your house that you might want to hide or get rid of, were Jesus to visit you in His physical body?
- What impact does a real belief in a risen Lord have on your children? What part do you play in their concept of who Jesus is?
- What impressions of Jesus do guests get from visiting your home? How can you strengthen this?

Option for Action
Think of creative ways that you can make the Living Jesus part of your family's daily life. Use your imagination, and enlist the help of all the members of the family. Some easy ways might include:
   a) having times of open prayer, speaking to God right in the room;
   b) making special worship habits for special occasions;
   c) reminding each other of Christ's presence when language or behavior does not honor Christ. (Do this not in a mean way, but lightly. The point is not to make an awareness of Christ an unpleasant thing!)

Take time at least to discuss the idea that, as a Christian family, you are part of Christ's family. Read the passage in John and tell your children about abiding and about life in a tent in Palestine in the time of Jesus (John 15:5–7). Give your children a chance to express what they think the verses meant to the disciples and what the verses mean to them.

Look Long, Follow the Steps

As Christian families, we are a people of vision and purpose. More than just an arbitrary mix of hormones, circumstances, culture, and timing, marriages and families given to God are ordained by God and designed to have a specific role in the world. Even if you married before you trusted Christ, He is still aware of all you are and can be, if you will look to Him with trust. Our children are "knit together in the womb" with a special purpose given by God, and we can teach this to all of them—whether they are biologically ours, adopted, or otherwise entrusted to our care. The Psalms teach that God's redemptive script for them is already written, no matter what the circumstances of their birth might be. In God's reality, there are no "mistake" people. Everyone has value and everyone has a purpose regardless of how they got here. God made us and knows us and sees us through.

The King James Version of Proverbs 29:18 states, "Where there is no vision, the people perish." The New International Version translates "vision" as "revelation." This concept also is true for families. If there is no hope, dream, or revelation from God about who you are to be as a family, serving God will deteriorate into empty ritual. God's plan for you and your family is the source of all motivation, decision making, and evaluation. The vision that God gives you frees you up to pursue not only the life that is most suited to you and your children but also the life that leads you to have the most powerful impact on the world around you. You are free to be yourself in the best sense of the word—without the hardness and scars and selfishness of an unredeemed life. You are free to serve the God who made you, knows you, and purchased you from your own sin with His own Son.

One of my hobbies is collecting published diaries of women who crossed the plains to help settle the American West in the 1890s. The hard work and deprivation of most of their lives was brutal, yet they wrote eloquently about the new life they had found and the joy they and their families had on the prairies. Most were women from middle-class, eastern, Protestant homes who were seeking a new, more idealistic life. While a twenty-first-century mind-set might think that these women were escaping religious and moral oppression in their established societies, the opposite was usually true. These women were more often (at least those who wrote diaries that have been found) seeking a new place to worship and practice their religion more devoutly rather than less devoutly.

The other amazing thing about the lives of these women is that they endured hardship after hardship—blizzards, death, floods, drought, danger from violent people, starvation—knowing that the homes they had come from were warm and safe and well provided for. The difference in their lives and in their families' lives?

It was a vision of a new life, the revelation that they had a purpose and a goal to achieve. This sense of moving forward made them strong and brave and gave their children a sense of being strong and brave as well. Mere self-interest is not enough to build a life on. God's purpose of "reconciling the world to himself"(2 Cor. 5:19 NIV) is enough.

Students on college campuses ask all the time, "How do I know what God's will for my life is?" Perhaps you are wondering now how to know God's vision for your family. Maybe you aren't married to someone very interested in God's vision for your family. Maybe you just don't feel any need to change things in your life right now. In any or all of these cases, the way to draw closer to God's vision and purpose for you is just to draw closer to God. Make an effort to know Him through the Scriptures, through prayer, through Bible studies and fellowships, just through silence. God is on your side and wants to show you and inspire you. Mostly, God just wants to be real to you and to be a presence in your life. That alone will fill your life with a sense of purpose and direction—the way you represent Him to the world around you. You needn't go any further than that to begin.

Are you parents who both agree that you want God's vision to live at your house? You're halfway there! You can begin the same way: Get to know God. Be thankful for all of your blessings. Learn a genuine worship, not just at church but also at home. Open up to God in every corner of your heart and of your hearth. Offer to God the best and worst of your family life and ask for His sweet healing. The vision of God can bring a sense of revival and renewal to you, your marriage, your children, and everyone who knows you. What an exciting prospect and daring venture. And God not only gives a vision, but lives with you Himself to carry it out. Purpose and vision will give your family a whole new dimension that will tie you together in new and healthy ways that will honor God and bring you comfort.

Consider:
- Think back on a time in your life when you worked toward a specific purpose or vision (perhaps as part of a drama or musical performance, a project at work, or reaching some desired goal). What was it like? Was there a special energy generated by the purpose you had? Do you recall the special feeling of accomplishment when you reached the goal?
- What do you consider your calling in your Christian life? Is this different from your "regular" life's calling? How could the two merge?
- If you know what calling and purpose God has placed on your life, how can you be sure that your family and home life fit in?
- What aspects of your family life can be brought more in line with what you see as God's purpose for your family?

Option for Action
Make a "date" like you made for determining family goals and values. Use the conclusions you came to from that exercise to help you seek God's vision. Find a time that you can have some fun marriage enrichment time,

as well as work out the direction you want your family to take. For example, plan for a baby-sitter and go out to eat; go to the beach while the children are at school; take a weekend away at a bed and breakfast. Find a relaxing "Sabbath" environment so that you will be relaxed and ready to joyfully listen to God.

Take your Bibles, and share Scripture verses that have been important to you and to your family. Share what they have meant in your life. Go over the family goals you discussed before. See if there are any connections with the verses you have found.

Take some time to pray together about all of the issues in your family life—the good, bad, and ugly. Commit all these things to God's care and love. Ask God to provide and guide the direction your family takes.

Separate and take some time to sit individually before God. Confess inner shortcomings and selfish thoughts and actions. Try to clear a path for the Holy Spirit to speak.

Come back together (maybe after a meal or a snack) and spend the rest of your time in prayer and discussion about what you feel God is leading you to do. Don't expect that in everyone's case God will speak in an "earthquake" way. Remember the story of Elijah and the "still small voice." Feel confident that you have opened your hearts and your life up to a new and exciting kind of leading from God. Be ready to hear His voice as you go about your daily life from now on.

More Real

Add your own list of insights for your Christian family. What other special strengths are yours because of Christ? Post them like banners around your house to remind you of whose reality you serve. The sense of being treasured that comes from knowing your home is special to God will give your children a sense of security that can't be matched by what the world offers.

Begin with Romans 12:1–2 (*The Message*): "So here's what I want you to do, God helping you: Take your everyday, ordinary life—your sleeping, eating, going-to-work, and walking-around life—and place it before God as an offering. Embracing what God does for you is the best thing you can do for Him. Don't become so well-adjusted to your culture that you fit into it without even thinking. Instead, fix your attention on God. You'll be changed from the inside out. Readily recognize what he wants from you, and quickly respond to it. Unlike the culture around you, always dragging you down to its level of immaturity, God brings the best out in you, develops well-formed maturity in you."

As you begin to work on your own truths and family values, take to heart the process of transformation that God is working in you. Don't rely solely on what someone else has taught you, or what the expectations of you are in your culture (even if you are in a "church" culture). Engage with the Living Lord, who has placed you in your family for that specific purpose for which you are striving. Make sure that your values reflect the values of the Scriptures.

Make some of the biblical characters your role models

as you seek out God's truths. Hebrews 11 is a great place to start. As you read over the list of faithful people, think of what you know about their lives. Some of them were killed. Some had no home. Some had to defy their culture and face ridicule and rejection. Be sure that the truths you build your family life on reflect God's view of the world, not a human view.

Families that are intentional about God's truth will be more ready to face both joy and crisis. Several years ago, a pastor and his family were traveling in a minivan when another car struck them head on. The pastor's wife and four of his six children were killed. As the news reporter interviewed the pastor, he asked, "How can you still believe in God after this happened?" The pastor replied, "This is exactly the time I must believe in God. This is what faith is all about."

Remember that just talking values and truth will not impress anyone, especially children. Your life must reflect what you believe about Christ, especially in behavior. Not that we are called to be perfect, or that our lives must repress all bad thoughts and actions. It is exactly the opposite! We are called to learn to repent, to be forgiven, to apologize when we are wrong, to be humble, to choose not to go against God. The overall truth of God's love and forgiveness can free us from being hypocritical and harsh to others, and harsh on ourselves.

The calling of God's truth is to be true, mistakes and all.

Consider:
• Who taught you most of the truths you would say you live by? Were they believers?

- What part of your Christian life is revelation, and what part has been handed down to you through your culture?

- Are the truths you teach to your children consistent with the Scriptures? Are you modeling them as well as speaking them?

- What one principle do you wish was more a part of your family life? What would it take for that to happen?

Option for Action

As you seek to be intentional about making your home a house of truth and a place that is real, find out what you can do to make these things real for your children. After you, as parents, have taken time away to seek out God's vision for you, take a weekend (or even a day) off as a "vision retreat" for your family.* List the godly values you want as the foundation of your home. Prayerfully consider other things that God may be showing you. Let your children, if they are old enough, express what they think are important values too.

Next, prepare an action plan for each of the values. Find ways that will make following God that fun adventure it should be. Remind yourselves that God is never stuffy or boring, and that He is waiting to do good things for you. Try to let go of family legacies that are from the world's culture and may block ways that God wants to lead your family. Be careful! God may give you adventures you don't expect, but God will always be working for your good and for His kingdom.

*If you are a single parent, or if your spouse is not a

believer or not completely sold out to following God, you can still seek God's vision for your life. More of the action plans will involve you alone, or you and the children. Your attitude will have to be like the husband or wife in 1 Corinthians 7 who wins over his or her spouse with a quiet and gentle spirit.

A Natural Pilot Project

F. F. Bruce, an author of books about the study of the New Testament, calls the church a pilot project for the kingdom of God.[2] Another natural pilot project for God's kingdom is the way that Christian homes work. All of our attitudes, our self-image, our views of others, and our original feelings about God are born within the atmosphere of our family. As caregivers and/or parents, so much power to set the tone for the world lies in our hands. With intentional family building under God's direction, we can begin to change the course of history.

Following Jesus' resurrection, He appeared again to His stunned followers and gave them a formula for what their mission on earth would look like once they had received the power from the Holy Spirit to follow Him. He gave them a geography for missions that at least in part is sometimes overlooked in today's missions efforts: "'You will receive power when the Holy Spirit comes on you; and you will be my witnesses in Jerusalem, and in all Judea and in Samaria, and to the ends of the earth'" (Acts 1:8 NIV).

Jesus' geography begins with "start at home." Our missions efforts anywhere can only ring as true as they are heard down the hallways of our own homes. Our churches too need to hear the gospel in some of their corners.

Children

A meeting for Sunday School teachers at one church included special training for leading non-Christians to know Christ. One young woman who was in charge of the preschool class sighed sadly, "I guess I'll never get the chance to share Christ with nonbelievers in my Sunday School class. All my children come from Christian homes."

"But, honey," a wise, veteran teacher told her, "none of your class members are Christians yet. You have more opportunities than anyone to share Christ!" With that, the young woman's countenance brightened.

"Wow! I've never thought of it that way," she exclaimed. The rest of the meeting she was totally plugged in and interested.

As you watch your own children play and grow and learn, remember that they will make their own personal decision about a relationship with Christ. Begin to pray now that any hindrances that might keep them from hearing Jesus' gentle calling to them would be removed. Ask God to help you as you lead them to know Him. Pray for a genuine, not forced, decision in your children's lives—according to God's timetable, not yours or that of your Christian friends. Let them know that God respects their choice to refuse Him if they aren't sure, and that He doesn't want some insincere decision they don't really believe in. Remove yourself as the motivation for some false gesture that has the potential of keeping them from hearing the calling voice of God in their lives.

Spouses and In-laws

Part of the most difficult calling as witnesses "in Jerusalem" involves presenting our love and commitment to Christ to our families, not only our immediate families but also those strangers who will be part of life for better or worse. One pastor's homily at a wedding ceremony tried to prepare the young couple for the realization that marriage is a totally unknown land. "One day," he preached, "you will wake up and see a stranger lying next to you in the bed." He wasn't speaking of a different person, but of the facets of that person's personality that wouldn't be revealed until some time into the marriage.[3]

In many cultures, marriage is arranged by parents, and the linking of families is part of a whole, bigger social structure. But choosing a marriage partner in a Western culture is more and more the total responsibility of husband and wife alone, and extended families must come along without input or consent. While the responsibility for choosing a spouse is freer to the individual, sometimes the relationships with extended family that go along with that choice makes life more difficult and less free. Fortunately, Christians who are making this choice under God's direction, or even those who have married without God's help, have all the resources of God to use their choice to lead people to Christ.

If a spouse and his or her family do not know God, the only healthy place to begin a Jerusalem witness is on our knees. The Apostle Paul is very specific about hanging in there with an unbelieving partner: "If any brother has a wife who is not a believer and she is willing to live with him, he must not divorce her. And if a woman has a husband who is not a believer and he is willing to live with her, she must not divorce him. For the unbelieving husband has been sanctified through his wife, and the unbelieving wife has been sanctified through her believing husband. Otherwise your children would be unclean, but as it is, they are holy" (1 Cor. 7:12–14 NIV).

The prayers and goodwill of the believer should be so compelling to the unbeliever that they want to repent and know God. Nothing is more valuable to unbelievers, their spouses, and their children than their turning from sin to embrace Christ. As Paul describes, their best chance for that is our love and our healthy life completely exposed before them. If we use their unbelief as an excuse to leave the marriage (barring any kind of abuse or infidelity), we haven't submitted that covenant of marriage we made with them fully to God. We should love them and cherish them and want their salvation more than anything else.

As we seek the salvation of a spouse we have committed to stay with for life, it is important to realize that our lifelong commitment in marriage extends also to that person's family—mother, father, sisters, brothers, everyone. God values each individual and seeks us to choose Him for ourselves; but that choice makes us part of the families and societies that God is seeking to build on the earth. We are never called on to be Lone Ranger believers just doing our own thing. At every step, Jesus encouraged His disciples to be engaged with each other and with the world in a way that brought the good news of Christ to more and more people. This must apply to believers and their families, especially those who don't know Christ.

Once again, the only way to begin to witness to those in your Jerusalem is on your knees in prayer. Just as it is important to really know your children when sharing Christ with them, it is important to know and clearly love the family that brought forth your beloved spouse. No true witness about Christ occurs apart from true love and concern for the object of that witness. Take time to know your spouse's family members and find ways to appreciate them as people. Be observant of what the family values and how their systems work. Humility will be a best friend in this endeavor. Imagine yourself in their shoes as you share Christ with them. In the power of the Holy Spirit, you will find that all your relationships, spouse and in-laws, will be easier and more encouraging when you are aware of this bigger purpose in your marriage and home.

Consider:
- On a scale of 1 to 10, how would you rate your relationship with your spouse? With your in-laws? (1 is nonexistent; 10 is fabulous)
- If your spouse's family members are believers, are there other extended family members for whom you can pray?

- If your spouse's family members are not believers, what will your prayer strategy be? Do you agree with 1 Corinthians 7? Do you disagree? Why or why not?
- What will you say to your children about Dad or Mom or grandparents who don't believe in Christ? How can you use the situation to help your children draw closer to God?

Option for Action

Assess the best long-term way to reach out to in-laws who are not believers or about whom you are not sure. Perhaps you just need to take time to get to know them better. How can you improve communication with them?

Remember that your marriage to their son or daughter may not have been in their plan of things. They may bear you some resentment and/or ill will. Your goal is to be Christ to them, not to be caught up in personality conflict or to nurse your own wounds and hurts. Study Matthew 5:38–42 and write down how it applies to your life in a bigger family.

NOTE: If you are part of a blended family because of death or divorce, you have even more of an opportunity to share Christ with a wider sphere. While your job may be tougher because of all of the hurts and scars of families that have torn apart and regrouped, you also have a more exciting and obvious opportunity to bring Christ's real healing to people's lives. As you seek Christ's light to dawn in each person in each of the family groups, remember that you are not alone and that God's abiding Spirit will teach you the most effective words and actions.

Family Members

Other fun places exist to begin a "Jerusalem" (i.e., "at-home") ministry that includes your children. Make a special time to pray together for family members (near and far), especially those who don't know Christ. This can be a time of real joy and common purpose. With your special care, teach your children not to be judgmental or haughty about others. Remind them that each of us was without God's salvation at some time in our lives. They can begin to have a sense of intercession for others that may be part of God's bigger plan for them. And what a joy when someone they know and love comes to know Christ!

Consider:

- How can you make your family's prayertimes consistent and fun?
- Do you have any baggage, or unforgiveness, toward your nonbelieving family members? What must you do to remove these barriers to prayer?
- How can you pray for your own children's hearts?
- What can you do to avoid a spirit of gossip, judgment, or condescension when you pray for others?

Option for Action

Regularly schedule a day (once a week? once a month?) for your "Jerusalem" project day. Decide together what you can do in addition to intercessory prayer as a missions ministry to someone in your immediate or extended family. Find ways for everyone to show kindness toward those you know don't believe. For example, older children can help serve the younger ones.

Begin a prayer chart for your Jerusalem efforts. This is exciting and lends a sense of continuity and momentum for children as it allows them to see what prayers are answered when! Your children's and your own faith will grow as you look back and see what God has done with your prayers.

---

[1]Sheila Upjohn, *Why Julian Now?* (Grand Rapids, MI: William B. Eerdmans Publishing Company, 1997), 131.

[2]F. F. Bruce, *The Message of the New Testament* (Grand Rapids, MI: William B. Eerdmans Publishing Company, 1972), 40.

[3]Christopher Graham, Church of the Savior, Roswell, Georgia, June 13, 1979.

6

Enlarging the Tent

The second part of Jesus' missions geography in Acts 1:8 challenged His followers to share what they had witnessed about Christ in Judea and Samaria. These were their nearest neighbors: one group just like them (the Judeans); and another group considered half-breeds, Jews who had intermarried with other tribes. Already, Jesus was shaking up the social system, changing the rules, and opening up opportunity for redemption to everyone. The Samaritans especially were not people who were traditionally invited to share in the salvation the Jews felt was theirs. They were the embarrassing "invisible" people of Palestine at that time.

Have you ever been employed in a service job—a housekeeper, a secretary, a nanny, a driver, a waitress, a cashier? Have you ever been part of a group where no one really knew who you were? If so, you can understand how awful it feels to seem invisible. As we teach our children about allowing God to use them to witness to others, we can teach them to recognize and respect people others might not even notice—the "invisible people." Our children can institute justice in a new way.

Muretus, a Christian scholar of the Middle Ages, traveled around Europe from library to library to study the Bible. He was poor and single, so he often looked unkempt and was homeless. But he really loved God. In one city in Italy he fell ill and was taken to a public hospital. As he lay on the surgical table, he heard the doctors gathered around him discussing his case in Latin. "What should we do with this worthless bum?" they asked, thinking he couldn't understand. "Maybe we can do some experiments on him."

The scholar, understanding perfectly, sat straight up and responded in perfect Latin, "Call no man worthless for whom Christ died."[1] Then he lay back down on the table to await their treatment.

As you minister to those close by, remember to look at people through Jesus' eyes, not society's. Your "Judeans and Samaritans," those who may not fit into your comfort zone, may be the people from whom you get the greatest blessing. Your children too may have a part in God's plan that brings redemption to people around you whom you never thought of helping. Be sure you encourage your children to listen to God about helping others. God is clear in His message to Isaiah about religion that overlooks people:

"'The multitude of your sacrifices—what are they to

me?' says the Lord. 'I have more than enough of burnt offerings, of rams and the fat of fattened animals; I have no pleasure in the blood of bulls and . . . goats. . . . Stop doing wrong, learn to do right! Seek justice, encourage the oppressed. Defend the cause of the fatherless, plead the case of the widow" (Isa. 1:11,16–17 NIV).

Once children are excited about how much God loves them and how blessed they are, they want to help others. Children and youth are terrific this way, and put adults to shame with idealism and enthusiasm! You can be the catalyst to help nurture in them a tender heart for others. This is the true beginning of missions—not some political stance or power trip. The missions message for Christian families is that they care and they will sacrifice to show that caring to others on the basis of someone's need, not on the basis of whether it is the right kind of person or not.

Help your children plan missions projects that include your neighbors and those who are in the same clubs, dance classes, sports teams, or even your church. The calling of Jesus to witness to the Judeans was a call to make your Christian commitment real in your everyday life. Rather than hiding out in church meetings, where everyone claims to know Christ, allow your commitment to truth and integrity to change the way your society and culture works.

These mercy ministries are very effective in sharing Christ with those "Judeans" who may see you every day or often but don't really know who you are. Christ's example of feeding and healing people all over Galilee and Judea gave people who knew of Him an idea of His purpose. It provided people with a glimpse into the goodness and the power of the God Jesus represented (and was). Notice as you study the Gospels that none of Jesus' acts of kindness (food, healing, forgiving, even raising from the dead) included a "hook." He didn't require people to convert to Judaism or even sign on as one of His followers. He merely expressed the nature of God by loving and giving to people. Their choice to follow came naturally out of experiencing that love, from their own initiative. Jesus never used kindness to manipulate.

As you teach your children to notice people around who need to experience the love of God, help to make this part of their understanding of God. You can use the practice of ministering to people around you to give them a sensitivity to others, as well as to teach them that it is Jesus Himself who draws people to salvation, not a preacher or a church worker or even them. Helping those around, Jesus must have known in His call in Acts 1 that sharing with people you live with every day is humbling and includes a built-in accountability.

Sometimes it is most difficult for us to share Christ with those to whom we are closest because they know us so well. Our own culture is the place to feel secure and affirmed, but it can also be the place where our weaknesses and foibles are known. Judea represented to those in Jerusalem the idea of cousins. The Judeans were relatives in the surrounding countryside, but were not immediate family. They most likely had much less sympathy for the wealthy people from the big city. Judeans were from the hills all around and may have even been hostile to the proud people of Jerusalem.

Whether you live in the city or the country, you can be the first in your neighborhood to break the system of geographical prejudice that Jesus addressed, and that we feel so keenly today. Make a point of sharing your faith with one of the people in your life who may feel invisible to others. Teach your children to appreciate all kinds of people, especially those who serve. They are following Christ by serving, and they will be first in God's kingdom.

Consider:
- How can you effectively teach your children to be "in the world, but not of it"?
- What do you see in the Christian community today that draws new believers to Christ?
- What do you see in Christian life that turns people away from Christ?
- How can your family be both accessible to others and true to Jesus' call?

Option for Action
Buy a map of your town or community. Lead your children to think about people they know or come in contact with who may not fit into their normal society, people who may feel invisible. Mark on the map where those people live, work, or go to school. As your family prays together, use the map to pray for the people God has brought to mind. Help your children think of ways they can help share Christ with those who may not

receive much recognition from the community at large. Encourage your children to think of this for their school friends too. The more the project touches their everyday world, the more they will learn from the action.

A *Different Kind of Politics*

The Samaritans—those not as "classy" as the Jews of the day—were another group Jesus mentioned specifically as being ones He wanted to hear the story of who He is. For us, this classification will vary from family to family and culture to culture. Perhaps for you as a child it would have been that little girl your mother wouldn't let you play with, that boy from the wrong side of town, or that snobby rich kid. That people who follow Christ will reach out beyond the human social norms and offer equal redemption for all is a world-changing concept. It is vital for families to open up to those who are different or uncomfortable.

Consider who represents Samaritans for you. An individual? A group of people? Is it racially based, like Jesus' day, or economically based? Are your "Samaritans" people with more or less education than you? Lead your children in praying for God's direction in ministering in a fun way to people around you. Find ways to short-circuit their expectations of people. Always be ready to listen to God's direction about helping.

Clarence Jordan, a Baptist writer and scholar from south Georgia, had a vision for translating the New Testament into language and images that were real for people in his own culture, not just for people in the Middle East. So, when he translated the Gospels and told the story of the good Samaritan, he set the story in south Georgia in the early 1960s. He had the travelers "going down to Atlanta," instead of Jerusalem. The Jews were white, and the Samaritan was black. While you may disagree with the idea of changing the Scriptures in this way, you can probably appreciate the sense of drama that the story would have had in the culture in which Jesus told the story. Racial hatred and violence were very real then, just as they are today. As you teach your children, with an eye to changing the world, part of what they need to learn is that God is not a "respecter of persons," and that they are related in sympathy and love to everyone God loves. By sending His disciples to the Samaritans, Jesus gave them an important lesson about "God's politics," which were very different from the politics of the Jews He grew up with.

Consider:

- None of us is without prejudice of some kind; but as followers of Christ, we are to let "all thoughts be captive" to Christ. What group is the most difficult for you to imagine loving? Can you turn those thoughts, day by day, over to Christ?

- Jesus' command is not just to not hate the Samaritans, but to witness to them, baptize them, and disciple them; in other words, to make them part of the church—your church. How will this be received at the place where you worship? Is God calling you to a different, more diverse kind of fellowship?

- How can you help your children overcome the

prejudices they will encounter in their everyday lives? Are there language and racial slurs that you can teach your children to avoid?

- How will you equip your children to deal with prejudice directed at them? Remember that Christ gives guidelines and help for those who are mistreated in society.
- Who are the heroes that you teach your children about? Are they a diverse group? Do your children know of heroes of the faith from different countries and different backgrounds?

Option for Action
Take time to talk with your children about prejudice and what makes it so wrong in God's plan for the world. Give them a chance to share with you what they think about others who are different. Make clear with them the distinctions between behavior and race; between actions one chooses and conditions one does not choose. Give them encouragement about who they are so that they can be confident and will not need to classify people unfairly.

Find "Judea" projects that you can do in the course of your regular routine. Are there people you see every day who could use a kind word or special recognition? What about the bus driver? Or the mail carrier? Or the grocery store clerk? All kinds of people in our lives need a glimpse of the gospel from us.

NOTE: There are also people who should *not* be part of the ministry that involves our children. You can use ministry projects with your children to help teach them to be safe and wary, "wise as serpents, gentle as doves." God would never call them into unsafe situations, and you can set down definite rules for helping others, such as:

1. Never try to help someone alone without an adult member of your family.
2. Never go anywhere with a stranger or get into a strange car.
3. Never give out your address or phone information.
4. Never do ministry without Mom's or Dad's permission.

Regular Encounters

Christians could have such an impact on the world if only they would begin to see the fun adventure of sharing Christ with the people around them. It is so easy to wait for a church-sponsored missions trip or an evangelistic crusade to begin to think of ways to share Christ's fabulous offer of new life. But God's Acts 1:8 plan is a brilliant way for Christ's followers to network with people they know. Think of the people you have the most influence on, people who trust you and with whom you have worked or played sports, or people you see on a regular basis. As you teach a missions heart to your children, help them to see that there should be something obviously different about a Christian. (For parents of teenagers, this difference is exactly what they don't want. Have grace and patience. They need to do their social developing.)

Be intentional about the way you treat the people you see on a regular basis. Your kindness and natural concern is enough to draw people to you. "Always be prepared to give an answer to everyone who asks you to give the reason for the hope that you have" (1 Peter 3:15 NIV). This is nothing like the American-culture stereotype of the "Bible thumper." Instead, this is the person who is generous, won't lie, doesn't strike out in anger, is sympathetic to others, and who has a humble and strong spirit. If you and your children project this spirit, you will never be short on people who want to know what it is you've got.

Another exciting aspect of God's purpose for you are those special times when He leads you into actions you would never think of on your own. Unlike the accidents of chance that rule the lives of unbelievers, yours and your family's mission is directed by a great God who steps into the workings of the universe to make His will known. Sound a bit grand? It's just what happens when you intercede in prayer for someone, or when you feel a special direction to send a check to someone, or when you make a meal for someone. God's "nudges" can lead you to work in some special way, the results of which you may or may not see.

In her book *Hidden Sorrow, Lasting Joy,* Anneke Companjen describes the experiences of wives of martyrs across our modern world. Over and over again, while their husbands were in prison, these women and their families were fed by God's own hand through the generosity of strangers who followed God's nudge. Many times, in Companjen's account, the source of the gift of money, food, or clothing could not be traced to any earthly connection. The Communists who were often the oppressors were always mystified and confused at how these women and their families survived. The supernatural work of God was too far outside of their belief system.

Another great testimony to the prayer work that God does in peoples' lives was the life of George Mueller. Although he was responsible for hundreds and hundreds of children in orphanages across England, he never once had to ask contributors for money. He simply prayed until God laid the children's needs on someone's heart.

Filling your family's life with an awareness of God's out-of-the-ordinary nudges adds to the great sense of adventure you want your children to have about God. Perhaps you have material goods, and God will gently guide you to share them with others (often in a way that ends up to be delightful). Or maybe God will call on some of your skills. At one church, a woman who knew how to bake pies taught this skill to others through the church's ministry to the homeless. Another young woman was a tap dancer who found God calling her to teach tap to some inner-city girls in an afterschool program. Another nudge from God was for an elderly woman to teach knitting to the little girls in a city shelter. They had only pencils for needles, but they took their knitting wherever they went and learned a new sense of pride in themselves and a gratitude to God for the woman who taught them.

Consider:

- As you pray about missions around you, what people groups will you focus on?
- Are there people you feel you can't minister to? Be honest with God and tell Him. It is part of our humanity. Ask God to help you to grow in this area.
- Make a list of the people you know you will encounter each week. With your children, begin your ministry by praying for each one. If you don't know their names, use one week just to find out names. Continue to pray.
- Try to prepare your heart for God's nudges. How do you normally hear God's voice in your life? Practice being open to God in little things so that you will be able to hear Him in the larger things.
- What will you teach your children about how God has miraculously provided for your own family? Are there areas to increase in faith, so that God can work?

Option for Action

A good way to begin your own intentional family ministries might be to read some of the stories and adventures of missionaries and other committed Christians. Nothing will inspire your family more than the stories of the way God has provided for others—both materially and with opportunities for service. Another good place to start is the Book of Acts. God did wild things—got people out of jail, sent help to Christians in need, and provided for the poorest churches. You can also tell your children the stories from your own family or friends in which God has provided and worked miracles. Videos like *The Hiding Place* and *Chariots of Fire* help show the adventure and excitement of following Christ. Give your children a sense that the culture in which they live has many misconceptions about following God. Ministry and missions are just the way to be part of the bigger, exciting thing God is doing in the world.

---

[1]William Barclay, *The Gospel of Luke*, rev. ed. (Philadelphia: Westminster Press, 1975), 16.

7

Beyond Our Borders

At a Christian convention during the height of the war in Afghanistan in 2002, a speaker made this comment: "We have all taken off our WWJD pins and put on American flag pins."[1] The comment gave many people pause. What would Jesus be doing in the face of national defense? How should we teach our children to treasure and defend their own country, and at the same time have a heart for missions and for "millions of people, groping in darkness"? You as a parent will have to think through what God is whispering into your heart. Review Galatians and Ephesians again. Read the end of Acts 1:8: "And to the ends of the earth." God desires for your family to have an impact on other places, whether through prayer, visits, or relocating there.

Prayer

Women of almost all Christian groups have a great legacy of prayer efforts, perhaps in part because of traditional roles that have limited their involvement in other arenas in the past. Prayer is a necessary underpinning for any missions effort and is itself a great missions activity. You can lead your children in a number of ways to learn to pray for missions and missionaries all over the country and the world.

As you catch a vision for what you and your family can do to support missions through prayer, make a plan for specific, regular, and consistent missions praying. Children of any age can participate and it can be a great learning tool. What fun to have a meal from a country for which your family will pray afterward. What a blessing for your children to realize how many people groups make up the country of Thailand or Mongolia. What a culture-changer it would be if all of the Christian children of one country felt they had a specific role in the lives of their brothers and sisters in another country. How peace could rule if we made an attempt through prayer to love and understand people from other cultures and ethnic groups. War and racial hatred and miscommunication would decrease so much if we had the courage to teach our children to pray regularly for people all over the world, even as Jesus commanded us to pray for our "enemies."

Prayer plays a huge part in the lives of Christian workers around the globe. Consider two young American women living in Afghanistan when war broke out who were captured by their hostile, terrorist enemies. Around the clock, and around the globe, Christians began to pray for them. Their own testimonies relate that they spent their time in captivity praying also. No doubt, it was not the beginning of a serious prayer life for them, but merely the continuation of it. In an amazing and miraculous way, they were rescued by removing the head scarves their captors had insisted they wear and burning them to signal their location to the American troops flying over. God's ear toward their prayers and the prayers of others opened that window for them to be rescued.

In teaching children about prayer, exercise special care and thoughtful explanation. The natural question children (and all of us, if we are honest) ask is, Why isn't everyone's prayer answered? For example, at the same time these two young women were being miraculously rescued, a missionary couple in the Philippines was being tortured and remained in captivity. (Later, in a rescue attempt, the man was killed by hostile gunfire, while his wife was wounded, survived, and was rescued.) A child's natural sense of fairness will ask, "Are they not praying enough?" or "Doesn't God love them as much as the other people?" If your children are your mission field, your own convictions about this question are very important.

Jesus answers Peter, who has a similar question, with a question of His own. Peter asks in John 21:21 (NIV), "Lord, what about him?" Jesus' response is, "If I want him to remain alive until I return, what is that to you? You must follow me" (John 21:22 NIV). Children need to know that God has a special and specific plan for everyone, but each person's journey with God will be different. Since He holds the key to death and resurrection, we are not bound to life on this earth the way unbelievers are. We can't pass judgment on God's plan, except to say that God wants everyone to know Him and experience His salvation through Jesus Christ. Your own trust in the goodness of God and your children's natural sense of fairness will make it clear that God does the best for us, even if others do evil.

Take time to pray for your children and their understanding and openness to God. Your children may have a better grasp on the ways of God than you just because they are so full of trust and idealism. Pray that God will give them clarity and a sense of His justice.

Consider:
- On what region of the world or country is God leading your family to focus your prayers?
- Is there a certain people group God is laying on your hearts?
- What about persecuted Christians living in countries with repressive governments? Are you brave enough to tell your children about what is happening to them? Can you express that God loves the persecutors as much as the persecuted?
- For what specifics can you help your children pray related to other people groups and other countries?

Option for Action
Record in a specific place the requests for which you and your family pray related to people around the world. Use magazine and newspaper articles and pictures from

the regions you have chosen to focus on. Guide your children in making specific requests, informed by their own (or your) research. If you have relatives in or from another country, let your children interview them about what the other country is like. Help them to feel a real tie to another place or people group so that they can really pray in love for them.

Cultures to Explore

Once you have established regular prayertimes in your family, an exciting next step is to begin to focus on a certain missionary, people group, region, or a particular type of ministry.

If there are missions education organizations in your church, be sure that your children are involved. If none exist, you may need to begin one or be the leader for your own children. Once you have begun a regular missions prayertime, you can easily transition also to a regular time to learn about missions around the world. Weekly, monthly, once a quarter, even once a year, a special missions learning experience will have an impact on the way your children view the world and the way they view God's love for the world.

Get excited about learning yourself. As you use this opportunity to teach your children about another culture or country, you also have the chance to build into them an appreciation for the goodness and mercy of God. Make sure that your examination of another culture is never condescending or judgmental. Teach your children the claim of Jesus that "whatever you did for one of the least of these . . . you did for me" (Matt. 25:40 NIV). That is to say that any missionary's work or prayers for the people in that culture are work and prayers for Jesus Himself. Keep in their minds that all cultures were lost cultures until the gospel entered them. And even Christian cultures only honor Christ to the extent that each individual honors Him. You have the power and responsibility to change some of the missions mistakes of past eras, both in the lives of your own children and in the kind of missions heart they will have when they are grown and serving God.

Be creative. Find missionary pen pals for your children. Better yet, missionaries' kids (MKs) might want to correspond with your children. Take a trip to the library to look up all you can about other cultures and regions. Make some sample native dress items for the children to wear. Find recipes from the area to try. Help your children make pictures or other artwork in the style of that region. There is no end to the things that can help your children learn to love another people group. At the same time, they will feel a part of a global world, being drawn closer by God's plan to reconcile everyone to Himself.

Going There

Although a missions trip is not always a possibility for every family, there are many ways to "put feet" to the missions concepts you teach in your home. More and more affordable opportunities for short-term trips arise all the time. Often it is the reluctance of the grown-ups instead of finances or schedules that keeps families from following God's call to the mission field, even short-term. We all for the most part end up doing what we want to do, or not doing what we don't want to do.

While my husband was in seminary, he learned this lesson very clearly. He was poor and the work was difficult and time-consuming. He felt that all of his free time and money were spoken for and he didn't think he could fit in one more responsibility. Then, we met and began to date. Suddenly, we both had time that we hadn't had before! We began to invest money we were sure wasn't there before on phone calls (we lived in different states). After some time passed, he even was able to buy a diamond engagement ring. We both learned that we were able to do the thing we were most passionate about, even if we wouldn't have admitted it before we met.

The same is true for missions, as well as for the life God has for you. The more you are passionate about Him, the more effort and resources you will put forth in serving and knowing Him. God will honor that and come to your aid.

Never underestimate the power of God to get you and your family where He wants you to go. Nothing else will galvanize the feelings of purpose in your family more than to actually go onto a mission field and serve. Or perhaps God is leading your family to help financially support a missions cause or a Third-World child through a reputable Christian organization.

For more and more churches, volunteerism and short-term missions projects have become an easier prospect. Families have found that hands-on work, as well as the adventure of travel and working with others, make God and church fellowship much more real. Try to find out what opportunities exist within the structure of your church and your denomination's missions activities. Be aware that full-time missionaries and mission-sending organizations have long-term strategies. Short-term volunteers need to be willing to fit into those long-term plans, not the other way around. The lesson in mission service is for your family to learn about service, not for the missions agency to learn a new way to do its work. Teach your children thoughtfulness and humility through exhibiting those traits yourself.

The key to missions being carried out in your home goes back to that ability to listen to God's voice and what part He has for you and your children to play in His plan. Frank and Edith Schaeffer, American Christians who were called to Switzerland to minister to college students there, had a unique prayer. They asked God to bring the people who were intended to help them at their chalet. But they also prayed that God would keep away those who would not help out the cause of Christ with them.[2] Pray for your family to be directed in exactly the way you should participate. Nothing short-circuits God's plan more than people doing simply what they think they ought to do. God needs people who will be obedient and do just what He tells them to do, in spite of what they feel. Show your children how you take time to listen to God and they will put that discipline into practice in their lives as well.

Consider:

- What kind of missions learning experiences do you like best? Are you communicating this to your children?
- As you refine your practice of missions praying and learning in your home, take some time to evaluate how it fits into the rest of your life. Is it consistent with the goals you have set for your family?
- How do you think a study of people in faraway places will change the dynamics of your family life (if at all)?
- What might you do to make these family missions prayertimes more fun and interesting? How can you keep this from becoming just a rote exercise?

Option for Action

Consider what God's call on your life really is. If your heart is unsettled and restless in your day-to-day job, consider the possibility of taking yourself out of it in order to serve God more completely. Be open to what God's wild adventure is for you as well as for your family. As you get caught up in the great stream of missions, you won't be able to be the same. Let God orchestrate the life your family leads on the earth and be confident that your family, surrendered to God, will change the world for the better.

---

[1]Tony Campolo, speaking at North Carolina Baptist Men's Convention, Charlotte, North Carolina, March 1–3, 2002.
[2]L. K. Parkhurst, Jr., *Francis and Edith Schaeffer* (Minneapolis: Bethany House Publishers, 1996), 91.

Epilogue
Letting Go

What a long journey you've had! As you turn to your checkbook and write out that check for the cap and gown rental, you can't help but think back to that first trip home from the hospital. Now, here are the same children, standing straight, fixing their hair, laughing, calling friends—getting ready for graduation. It's a breathless moment for a parent, exhilarating and frightening at the same time. Did I do enough? Will they make good choices? Will they follow the rules? Will they love God? All of that sense of responsibility and adventure has percolated down to this one moment. Soon you will get to see exactly what kind of adults your children will become.

As you prepare for your children to leave the nest, prayerfully consider what new role you will have in their lives as young adults. Think back to examples in your own life. What did your parents do that was most helpful to you as you began your own young adult life? What advice and participation from your parents was not helpful? What things were constructive? What was destructive? Genetic makeup as well as the psychology that God put into human beings often leads people unknowingly to "become" their parents. This is not always a bad thing, but to repeat patterns unconsciously without being intentional about behavior can be.

For example, one man repeated the pattern he had so resented in his father. As a middle-aged man, the father had begun an affair with a much younger woman, left the family in tough circumstances, and proceeded with a messy and unhappy divorce. The son, dealing as best he could with the hand he was dealt, made his own way as an adult. He married, raised a lovely child, and worked hard. But when the child turned 18 and left for college, some restlessness began to stir in him. He began to resent the confines of his long-term marriage. He became unwilling to seek counsel or help. As his child moved through college, this dad's relationship with his wife became less and less appealing, until one day they agreed that divorce was the only option. A few months later, he moved in with a much younger woman who was raising three small children by herself. His adult child was left to deal with much of the same pain and discontinuity that he had dealt with as a young adult himself.

While this example seems extreme, there are many extreme patterns buried deep in our psyches. Our parents, for good or for bad, are the parenting models imprinted in our minds. "Much evil is not done by evil men, but by good men who do not know themselves,"[1] said one

American thinker. Parents who know themselves better through prayer and through examining the lives and habits of their own parents can establish a better bond between themselves, their adult children, and their grand-children. As you let your children go and grow, be intentional and know yourself. Let God be the author and finisher of their faith. Your part as a main player is done.

The Bible points us to this difficult two-sided coin. Remember that God's initial promise of salvation came to Abraham in a generational way. "I will bless you and your children and your children's children. Your descendants will be like the stars and the sand" (Gen. 32:12, *author's paraphrase*). God knows that healthy family and godly par-enting make up the building blocks that allow society work in the best possible way. If all of the parents down the line from Abraham had been faithful to God and the rules for healthy life He gave Moses, what a different world would exist now.

But the Bible also knows the reality of selfishness and sin. "'The parents have eaten sour grapes, and the chil-dren's teeth are set on edge'" (Jer. 31:29 NRSV). Just as healthy and wholesome families pass down legacies of secure, happy children, unhealthy and dysfunctional fami-lies pass down the difficult and ugly parts of their relationships. Most families pass down a little each of good and bad. Only through the grace of God can the unhealthy patterns be short-circuited, and God can only work through those who are intentional and conscious of taking new and positive paths.

As you consider your new relationship with these new, independent persons, consider these things. First, God loves them even more than you do and will be more effective at leading and guiding them, especially out of difficult and/or sinful situations. "You can't nag someone into heaven," you may have heard someone say. You will need the same total trust in God you had when your children were vulnerable infants.

Second, both you and your children may need a new kind of distance between you. They need a chance to try their wings and perhaps make some mistakes. Otherwise, they will never have the confidence they need to learn to be productive and strong for God. You also need a chance to step back. As a parent, you can no longer be the emotional support for your children. They will need to search for that elsewhere, hopefully in God. It is not healthy for your marriage or your own relationship with God to still be living for your children after they are grown. It is like never letting your children take off the training wheels of their bikes or making them wear water wings even after they learn to swim. It is embarrassing for all of you. You have a great opportunity to turn your creative and loving attention toward your other children, your spouse, and even God and your relationship with Him.

Third, while some of the other responses seem like a pulling back, your prayer life can see a great advance. You have a wonderful place in God to aim all of your parenting energy that is no longer focused on your children's day-to-day life. You can become a fierce prayer force, remembering to bring before God all of the worries you have, all of the petitions about your children's spiritual life, even about your children's future. God loves when we pour our hearts out honestly, even to complain and vent.

Fourth, find new channels for that loving and nurturing parent impulse. Teach a children's class in Sunday School. Volunteer to be a mentor or a tutor at your local school. Offer to baby-sit for some young couple in your church. There is never a shortage of children who need love, and unselfishly loving someone else's children is a continuation of the way your family will change the world. Pray for God to clearly give you opportunities to serve Him with the parenting impulses you may still feel.

Fifth, renew your own spirit by turning back to things you may have put on hold since you had children. Do you paint? Begin a new try at painting. Do you love to cook? Try those recipes that the children would never eat. Give yourself time to relax and reflect on things. Become more involved in the ministries of your church. Make new friends. Allow God to use the freedom you feel to make you a better and more balanced person, the best thing you can be for your adult children. Remember, you are the template they have for parenting.

Thank God for the opportunity to be a parent and for the next phase of becoming friends with your young adult children. Ask Him to give you wisdom, patience, and faith that His word will "never return void."

---

[1]Reinhold Niebuhr, quoted by William Smith in a sermon at 19th Avenue Baptist Church, San Francisco, California, 1983.

Appendix A
Missions Projects to Your Children

With such a vital and exciting task, first to introduce your children to God and second to let God use your family in His grand scheme of reconciling the world to Himself, every parent needs to make an intentional and thoughtful effort to help usher children into the new world that is the kingdom of God. Parents can no longer expect that culture (schools, government, civic societies) will build Christlike principles into children's lives. Nor can believers today rely just on church, children's programs, youth groups, and Bible studies to live out for children the great Christian faith adventure. Too many forces can pull them in other directions—television, pop culture, and a materialistic lifestyle, to name a few. If children are to be safe and comfortable in the world and not of it, they need to know for themselves how good and loving the God who made them is.

Here are some ideas for helping teach your children that God is not only true but also loving and fun.

1. Have a Jesus and art search.

Take your children to the closest art gallery. Look for old masters paintings that often have Christian or biblical themes. Talk with your children about the artists who took God seriously (for example, da Vinci, Rembrandt, and Cezanne). Challenge them to search the art gallery for pictures of Christ on the Cross, other stories from the Bible, or art from churches.

Even if the art is all modern art, let your children talk about what they see and how it relates to God. Most artists want to present ideas and philosophies. Even the most unappealing painting or sculpture can help you guide your children toward thinking about God.

Make note of concerts and performances offered in your area. Many works of classical music have religious themes and/or were written by devout Christians. Find a way to help your children learn about heroes of the faith who were musicians and composers. Let them know that believers can feel proud of the way that God changed the world in the past through what artists, musicians, and writers did.

2. Invite exciting and interesting Christian brothers and sisters into your home.

At some point, it is healthy and important for your children to find role models outside of home. Rather than let that float along arbitrarily, intentionally invite younger and "cooler" people into your home; people who have great testimonies and who love God. Let your children know that they, or you, aren't carrying out an isolated, Lone Ranger task. God has a fun and exciting network of people who are part of His plan, and the people God calls represent a great diversity.

3. Rather than disdain and criticize modern culture, help children explore it for Christ.

One of the best things my children ever received was a cassette tape of a Christian rap band. They were introduced to God in a style that they liked, rather than my musical taste ruling the day and them thinking that God only likes old, tired, "unhip" music. The Christian music world has exploded with all kinds of styles and rhythms. Though not quite at the same level yet, Christian-based films and television shows are beginning to be produced with more integrity. Like art, some films bring up themes for which Christianity has the answer. A variety of magazines, especially the ones for teens, can help children feel a sense of connectedness with their culture. Children in the world but not of it will have a much better chance of carrying the message for Christ than children of the world but not in it. Children who never learn to love God's creation and all of the people in it, who fear everything and everyone outside of their limited Christian world, will grow up to be adults who isolate themselves, mistrust others, and cause great hostility and division among peoples.

And those children who rebel and leave a sheltered Christian nest may never feel that God could use them because their tastes and approaches differ from their parents' and maybe, they feel, from God's. What a shame that as adults they may stay alienated from God just because they were never introduced to a God who loves them no matter what their style!

4. Have a regular, set time to spend listening to and respecting your children's ideas—especially their ideas about God.

An FBI chaplain from Oklahoma City whose specialty is trauma and violence once said, "What a victim doesn't need from a counselor is someone with a better story." This is also true for children as they try to think life through and begin to own their own ideas and thoughts, especially about God. Sometimes in parents' eagerness to make sure that children get it right, they stifle the way God might be working in the children's minds. Parents have a way of wanting to have a better story to share with their children about Christ in their lives. But often what children need is to express their own ideas and feelings. Sometimes it doesn't really matter what the specifics are, just that there is an adult who will listen to them seriously and respectfully.

5. Show your children the wonderful world God has made for them.

Take to heart Paul's claim in Romans 1:20: God is making Himself known to people through His creation. With your children along, explore all of the wonders that God has placed around you—flowers, trees, caterpillars, stars, the sea. All children are fascinated with life and living things. From their earliest ages, help your children know how special they are to God and how God made all the wonders of the universe for them to enjoy and explore. Share with your children the high value God places on life, especially human life, and how important they are to God.

Take family field trips to different areas with different ecosystems. Help your children think of ways we as believers can be more responsible in helping keep the earth clean and working well. A great gift to them is an appreciation for what God made in the state that He made it. On your trips, spend time in worship and praise to the God who made the lovely earth.

6. Share your own journey and the journeys of your believing family with your children.

Perhaps the most effective tool that God has given to you to use for ministering to and sharing with your children is your own story. According to what is appropriate for their age, take intentional and specific time to share with your children exactly how God had an impact on your life and at what point you turned your life over to Him. If you are not sure about this, write the story out for yourself. If you can't, make an appointment to talk with a pastor or Christian friend about it.

As you share with your children, (1) don't assume. Don't assume that they know what church words and religious language really mean, even if they have heard it all of their lives. Be clear and use language that they will understand. (2) Don't try to dress up your experiences or sanitize what you were like before you met Christ. While it may not be appropriate to tell all, you can share your feelings and the rebellion that perhaps was in your heart before you met God. Your admission of sin and brokenness gives the glory to God in your life. And it gives your children a way to deal with the wrong that they know exists in their own lives. A Christian witness that only glorifies the action of the believer doesn't give the glory to Christ. As you witness to your children, let them know that you were different after Christ saved you.

Appendix B
Missions Projects with
Your Children

A s your children grow, they will be more and more interested in helping others, whether or not they have made personal commitments to Christ. Children pass through significant learning stages as they grow and mature, and at each stage, helping others can be fun for them and can be a significant part of the learning that guides them the rest of their lives. With your example of an attitude of love for others and a sense of purpose and calling for your family, missions projects can provide family enjoyment and bonding experiences that instill in your children life skills that enable them to help.

1. Find local ways to help local people.
Just like Jesus' command, think about your "Jerusalem" for your first focus. It seems incongruent to expend great cost and care for people far away from you and your family with

whom you have no relationship, while neighbors just blocks away may be in need.

One enterprising mother simply used her swimming pool as a local ministry tool. By being open and friendly to neighbors and their children, she found that most of the children on the block ended up at her house swimming on hot summer days. The parents were relieved to have the children out, but safe. As this mom looked around her, she began to recognize the great ministry opportunity that was literally in her backyard. Most of the children were from families that did not attend church, or at best attended only nominally. Through the normal, Christian lifestyle of her and her children, the other children from the block were able to see a new way to think about God and Christianity.

Jerusalem opportunities are all around us, if we will prayerfully look. Every community has a nursing care or assisted living facility. Call to find out what you and your children can do to be helpful. Make an art or craft project or take small potted plants to give to the people who are bound to institutions. One teacher of a teenaged girl's Sunday School class takes her girls once a month to polish the fingernails of the women in a retirement facility. You might also call a local community center or mission. Ask them what help they can use and whether the tasks or situations are appropriate for children the ages of your children. Remember the old proverb, "Don't scratch where it don't itch." Each mission or mission church or church's mission will have specific things it needs and specific things it doesn't need.

Take care in training your children to be helpers, not

just do-gooders, especially where other full-time ministers are involved.

2. Teach your children at home about children around the world.

There are many ways to get children involved in thinking about other countries and other peoples around the world, and their awareness and excitement builds in them an openness that God can use to pursue His purposes around the globe. Concentrating on different cultural aspects of people's lives but teaching clearly how many similarities all people have will do a great deal for peace and a caring attitude toward others. Find out ways that other cultures have benefited society and what in the history of other peoples is admirable and noble. We need not repeat the mistakes of the past carrying our nationalism and prideful culture to other countries. God needs people who will go, care for, and love people; and maybe give their lives for their friends just as Christ did.

Some specific ways of getting a taste of another culture include:

- Cooking dishes from that country or culture.
- Going to a restaurant that serves that kind of food.
- Going to the library to look up fun facts and information.
- Emailing missionaries in those places.
- Looking for pictures of the clothing of that country and making up clothing that is similar.
- Looking online for information and pictures.
- Finding a safe pen pal from another country or culture for your child. (Work through your church or

your denomination's mission-sending agency to do this.)

The possibilities are only as limited as your imagination. Perhaps there are cultures close to home that you and your children can visit. Nothing helps to reconcile the world to God and to itself more than the friendships between children and youth.

3. Become a missions education leader at your church or in your home.

Some larger denominations and Christian publishers offer curriculum materials to teach children and others about ministries and missions efforts across America and around the world. If your church does not have an ongoing missions education program for children and youth, talk to your pastor about helping to begin one. If that is not possible, check a Christian bookstore for missions education materials you can use with your children at home.

Set a set day and time so that your teaching will be consistent, and make it as much fun as you can. Children will get excited about praying for others; they will feel part of a bigger purpose; and they will learn that the world is a much bigger and more interesting place than just their town or their block. It will also help them to move more smoothly into ministry projects, enjoy the thrill of helping others, and see people come to know Christ through their efforts.

4. Start a structured and consistent prayer ministry.

Often we overlook one of the most powerful ways to bring about change in the world because it requires the fewest materials and equipment. The undergirding of prayer is perhaps God's most important channel in changing the world, yet Christians sometimes relegate this important task to the nonactive category. What a great influence you can be on your children if you start teaching them to pray about everything when they are young. Another powerful witness to prayer is having a regular way to record what you have prayed and then the answers to your prayers. Nothing influences children more than the specific, tangible proof of God working in their lives and in lives around them.

Posters, notebooks, journals—any way that you decide to help your children record this new serious prayer life can be a creative and stimulating activity they help shape. If they design their own poster, notebook, or journal, for example, then their prayers take on more of the flavor of their personalities. As you walk through this prayer activity with them, guide them into a deeper prayer life. Prayer is more than just a wish list. Prayer for the well-being of others, perhaps at the sacrifice of something they wanted; prayer for world leaders and world situations; any and all prayer confirms in children and in parents that they are not powerless and that their time spent in prayer has an impact on God's plan for the universe.

5. Try your hand at a Judea or a Samaria ministry.
With your children, try to think of ways your family can contribute in ministry to the people who may have been forgotten or neglected in your community. A popular term for this is "practicing random acts of kindness."

Make it more fun for children by characterizing it as a "secret conspiracy" to help people without their knowledge and without a reward for them. Remind them that God, "who sees what is done in secret, will reward you" (Matt. 6:6 NIV). (Some translations include "openly.")

As you do these ministries, try to make it a point to be helpful to a variety of people. Don't only help people exactly like you. Encourage your children to enjoy helping all people and remind them that this is a part of your witness for Christ. Before you go out to help, practice answering the question of why you are helping—for the sake of Christ.

6. Explore the holidays in a new way.
On holidays that involve giving and/or receiving presents, especially Christmas, you and your family can add a new dimension to the traditional, materialistic, consumer culture. Find ways to simplify what your family does for each other; and let creative, rather than financial, powers rule the day.

Remind children that the tradition of gift giving, especially at Christmas, began as a recognition of the gift that the wise men gave to the baby Jesus, and the gift of salvation that Jesus gave to all of us. In other words, the tradition comes from the joy of *gift giving* rather than *gift getting*. Take back the holiday from the consumer society that we live in and lead your children in new and fun ways of giving to others in the spirit of Christ. Make an adventure of giving to those who may not receive very much.

Thanksgiving also began with Christians being

thankful to their God for helping them survive the harsh winter. It was also a time of racial reconciliation between the Native Americans, without whose help the Pilgrims would not have survived. As a ministry from your home, invite someone who might be lonely or hurting to share in the bounty your family has. Think especially of those who are visitors in our country. Through your generosity you can change the world by reaching out to those who are here from other countries and may not otherwise be exposed to the gospel of Christ.

Suggested Reading

Blackaby, Henry T., and Kerry L. Skinner. *Called and Accountable*. Birmingham, AL: New Hope Publishers, 2002.

Blackaby, Henry T., and Claude V. King. *Experiencing God*. Nashville: LifeWay Press, 1990.

Chesterton, Gilbert K. *Orthodoxy*. New York: Dodd, Mead and Company, 1908; New York: Doubleday, Image Books, 1990.

Companjen, Anneke. *Hidden Sorrow, Lasting Joy: The Forgotten Women of the Persecuted Church*. Wheaton, IL: Tyndale House Publishers, Inc., 2001.

Cronin, A. J. *The Keys of the Kingdom*. Boston: Little, Brown and Company, 1944; Boston: Little, Brown and Company, 1984.

Dawn, Marva J. *Keeping the Sabbath Wholly*. Grand Rapids, MI: William B. Eerdmans Publishing Company, 1989.

Heschel, Abraham Joshua. *The Sabbath*. New York: Farrar, Straus and Giroux, 1951; New York: Farrar, Straus and Giroux, Noonday Press, 1975.

Lewis, C. S. *The Great Divorce*. 1946. Reprint, San Francisco: HarperSanFrancisco, 2001.

Omartian, Stormie. *The Power of a Praying Parent*. Eugene, OR: Harvest House Publishers, 1995.

Peterson, Eugene H. *Living the Message*. Edited by Janice Stubbs Peterson. San Francisco: HarperSanFrancisco, 1996.

Smith, Hannah Whitall. *The Christian's Secret of a Happy Life*. Westwood, NJ: Barbour Books, 1985; Uhrichsville, OH: Barbour Publishing, Inc., 1998.

Chapman, Gary. *The Five Love Languages*. Chicago: Northfield Publishing, 1996.

Chapman, Gary, and Ross Campbell. *The Five Love Languages of Children*. Chicago: Moody Press, 1997.